SOUTH OF HEAVEN, NORTH OF HELL

DAVID LYNN BAILEY

TABLE OF CONTENTS

To Donna, my muse and wonderful wife.

And to my mother, who always had urged me to write. Also I give thanks to my friends and family who supported me with praise and encouragement.

But most of all it is to God and his glory, who gave me the words, and to whom I thank the most.

Mothers, Fathers and Children...

A Cradle of Arms

If I could be held in a cradle of arms
In a haven of safety, of motherly charms
Forever and ever, I'll long to stay there
There in the heaven my mother would bare

If I should be caught in the whirlwind of war
I'll call for your loving, so I may endure
And straight through the tempest your tears would then breach
Singing and crooning in a mother's soft speech

If love should be taken away from my heart
With nowhere to end and nowhere to start
So quickly you'll gather me close to your breast
Where hearts can be mended with love that is best

If I should be bound to a mountain alone
Beyond a friend's shoulder, beyond who I've known
My cry for an answer would not go unheard
For there in my memories, my mother was stirred

If all of my years should come and go by
Please let me recall in that blink of an eye
The cradle my mother would comfort me in
And know that I'll join her real soon once again

A Mother's Dream

How did this come to be
My daughter who is so grown up
Whose light out brightens me

For none could hardly know
That when I was, what you are now
My light had yet to glow

Mistakes I've often made
And had to learn through every one
And every one I've paid

Yet you somehow had found
A shortcut through the learning years
To life's maturing ground

So often I would pray
That all my faults and falls I've had
Would not upon you, prey

Yet this I must have stressed
You dearly are a mother's dream
For which I'm truly blessed

So take this gifted start
That God has given you to have
And all my love to heart

Baby

Oh breath of life, how clear to me
Your tiny chest beats peacefully
Upon my face as I draw near
I feel your breath, so soft and dear

Your eyes are closed in restful sleep
As you lie still without a peep
So precious in just what you are
More pleasing than a wishing star

Your little cheeks cry out to me
To place my lips down onto thee
So as I draw my face to yours
I barely hear your feeble snores

What joy has come to claim my eye
In watching you, my apple pie
Then gently will your mouth twitch some
To come to rest upon your thumb

I reach to touch your curly hair
So smooth and soft, so fine and fair
Oh breath of life, the years have gone
Yet memories I still dwell upon

Of all the years I've looked back to
They all were filled with love for you
But never would I see again
That moment where you once began

Letting Go

What calling did you hear
What summoned you to turn about
To walk the road from here

Why is it, I can't too
Is this just something only meant
For growing youths like you

What flaw has nature weaved
That home should be a starting point
To places yet perceived

Will love be just a dream
When you move on beyond my arms
And drawn away downstream

Remember from the start
That all beginnings have an end
But ne'er a mother's heart

Hold fast from doing wrong
Hold fast to what you know is right
And may your love be strong

But one thing you must do
And that's to always carry forth
My love as part of you

Shun not this empty nest
For never will you be without
A place where you can rest

Like You

What world would I now deeply hold
With truths I did not see
If not for all that you had told
From father's love to me

What road in life would I not fear
With choices unafraid
Had I not you to steer me clear
Of trials that life had made

This man in life that I've become
In values I'd been clad
Had only been imparted from
My idol, I call dad

What apple of a parent's eye
Could truly be set free
When knowing that its fall will lie
Right next against the tree

So no matter how you measure
My father through and through
It is his love I'll treasure
With this need to be like you

Mom

She never had to stand before the ram
Defending her young from what harm may come
She only knew the life as a lamb
And the joy of her children, and then some

She never thought to want tomorrow
Because it was enough to have each day
She lived on the smiles, but never the sorrow
And wouldn't consider, any other way

She never expected to be rewarded
For all that she did was ample enough
She had always found, a way to afford it
Anytime that her young, had needed stuff

She never steered us from our dreaming
For dreams were the fountain that sprang all hope
She simply showed that there was meaning
Upon life's road and treacherous slope

Within my heart I hold the answer
To the many things she had taught me of
But the greatest thing I've learned from her
Was the capacity to show my love

The Tines of Fate

Oh my daughter, what a cruel world this can be
For time and again, you found yourself beaten down
And left upon the walking plank, inches from the sea

Oh how the coffers of your golden heart, been emptied out
Drained away by the madness of your insipid days
And leaving you abandoned with your spirit in full rout

My dear, dear daughter, how I weep to see you at a loss
I watch your pain grow steadily, as it envelopes you
While tightly binding you within, to hang upon your cross

What justice has befallen you, to bear this living woe
What failing had we all induced, for heaven to let go
And what help could I in all my prayers, could heal the heart I know

Oh my fated daughter, the tines are truly running deep
Tilling your life beyond all likeness, of that which was before
While giving you resting only, in the halls of any sleep

Oh how the hue of life, been so diluted or sweat away
Each day's a day of constant struggle and hidden tears
While hope will linger somewhat, like the sun's last glowing ray

Take hold my daughter unto my trembling, supporting hands
For I will always stand by you, you, my golden heart
And offer all my love can give, as long as time demands

When Hearts Bespoke of Weariness

Whenever the earth grows wicked
Where no foot can hold its ground
That's when our world's restricted
And no longer safe or sound

For such a night awaking
Can cause many to despair
It'll send some hearts to breaking
With their lungs to gasp for air

Such is the realm of living
Where our follies can and may
Impair our days by giving
Us the wounds that fall our way

Fear not my gentle daughters
From the hounds of hell in life
But seek more calming waters
Than the stormy shores of strife

For worlds do come asunder
And our dreams can fall apart
But never doubt or wonder
Of a father's loving heart

Nature...

Bluebird

Oh bluebird, thou art a heavenly thing
Thy realm does lie among the clouds
Thy song is filled with spring

Oh bluebird, your wings beat only love
And fills the wind that touches all
Down to us from above

Oh bluebird, such is thy magic way
For seen but once within our sky
Will cause our hearts to sway

Oh bluebird, what wonders fill your eye
You sit upon God's window sill
And watch the angels fly

Oh bluebird, you're there when lovers wake
You are the first whom they will see
When morning comes to break

Oh bluebird, it's hope your voice would sing
And hope that I will always see
The hope you sing each spring

Mountain Magic

There is no mountain snow clad peak
That can't be reached by man
Such is the life that all men seek
To climb what loft they can

No icy perch or virgin height
Will still their lust to try
They'll climb in spite of day or night
Wherever they should lie

Such beauty men are so drawn to
These snowy regal gowns
It's how they rule a sky so blue
Majestic in their crowns

But let it not be said that all
Were climbed for just conquest
For most were climbed so they would fall
In love, at very best

Pearl

What ageless beauty hath the pearl
Attired in heaven's creamy white
Such purity it would unfurl
With a grace that brightens any night

To think that it had come from naught
And only grew where darkness keeps
While sleeping long in lonely plot
Sustained by tears, the keeper weeps

What passion doth the pearl unlock
Whene'er the eye would come to meet
Twill in that moment pause the clock
And any heart it's precious beat

For had not Helen dazzled Troy
And had not sunsets swept the skies
So too the pearl whom hearts enjoy
A treasure that the world would prize

Snow

Down from a gray hedonic sky
Tumbling like pieces broken from heaven
Pristine, pure and blithely simple
It's mesmerizing to my thirsting soul

Like an army of little angels in fluffy white gowns
They seek to exalt the glory of winter
To watch them is all and everything
With a silence transcending the barriers of living

For God's perfect peace has never been nearer
As in the glorious moment of each falling flake
So quickly they clothe the autumn's last colors
Putting them to sleep beneath blankets of white

Thus deep and deeply the earth takes its rest
As do the bears within their dens
All would now wait through the cold and the bitter
Until the robins come calling again in the spring

Sunflower

Behold a golden flower
That stands so tall in basking sun
Like heaven's little tower

So bright in red and gold
So cherished by the bumblebee
So beautiful and bold

It stands so regally
And holds its face unto the light
Where God can speak to thee

No garden could hide you
No earthly wall or border fence
Can keep you out of view

The valleys sing your praise
And meadows yield their beds to you
Where angels stop to gaze

Such glory and vast power
From longing eye to beating heart
Within this bright sunflower

Taken to the Sky

I spied you from afar
Whose beauty grew within my sight
Like any evening star

So stunned, I did not see
The other stars that loomed about
So awed I was of thee

Oh treasure of the sky
Who fills me with this calming ease
The triumph of my eye

So captured by your light
That all my dark was whisked away
As though it wasn't night

Such was my heart's desire
To watch you dance across the sky
Like passion's sparkling fire

Bring forth your magic dust
So we may dance together there
Transform me, that you must

The Play

Inhale the pageant of the night
Those countless stars that spin delight
Like heaven's little wildflowers
That charms and sparkles, souls to its light

Ever the road leading hearts away
This celestial parade, this cosmic play
That pulses with a living beat
Sublime and hypnotic, in stately sway

Such is the curtain dressed in black
This veil of splendor on starry rack
I hang upon that astral web
Ensnared by threads, by stars I track

This night, each night, I seek this page
And yearn to step onto that stage
To see each star a breath away
Sprightly alive and timeless in age

Life...

A New Year

Has your year been going badly
Has it made you more than blue
Has the world been turning madly
From the ways that you once knew

Can you see the sun arising
Can you hear the rolling thunder
Can you feel the world a turning
Does it stand to any wonder

Are there roads that lead to nowhere
Are there streams that flow uphill
Are there skies that see no sunshine
Does it stand to any ill

Is the wind the only whisper
Or the cold the only chill
Is the rain the only moisture
Must we stand for all this still

So let not the weather throw you
Keep the bee outside your ear
And if your cookie still would crumble
Then there's always a new year

Choices

Folly lives within the shadow of commonsense
A chimera pretending to display its wit
And when a man seeks out the wisdom that he needs
He could instead, be engaged with the counterfeit

Man lives within the concept that he can't be wrong
And names it anything but what it should be called
Such hubris is the maiden spawn to even more
And the keystone upon which our fallacy's sprawled

Choices lie at the very heart of all we do
With consequences weighing in, within its wake
For every turn in life, another had been missed
With opportunity or a mishap at stake

Wherefore are the values that a man can use
To aid him in dilemmas that he'll come to face
Is his soul infused upon the horns of conceit
Or, is humbleness and humility in place

Clarity

In clarity's brief second
It can eradicate the past
Like a flood washing over
The beliefs we held fast

Upon the pyramid of our thoughts
Designed to wick away the slinking
Of life's foolish ideas
From the apex of our thinking

Perceptions are colored
By a heart's thirsting need
How we view any knowledge
And how we take, and concede

Sometimes in a moment
When our vision becomes clear
Through the shroud of spent logic
A truth will appear

In clarity's brief second
The world had been turned
What we once thought was clover
Had been torched, and been burned

Digs

Insult to injury, it can't be denied
Like a whirlwind of chaos, the words can not hide

Where prudence craves weather, that's sunny and bright
It's the storms in our living, will undo what is right

We have a secret desire, whenever we're mad
For a final last thrust, with words that we add

So how can we tether, the devil's sweet glee
To refrain the mad hatter, from talking crazy

It's heartless unthinking, with salt in our hand
To be callously tossed, in wounds where they stand

Is deception the way, we do what we do
By fooling our thinking, then claiming it's true

In our conscience domain, where justice is served
Can the rights of the better, be truly observed

What selfless endeavor, could we aspire to
To hold back the sniping, and quips that we hew

Must meanness be ever, a state chose to live
Or can we be bigger, and learn to forgive

Encumbered One

Has love's bright star, brightened less
To shimmer in new doubtfulness
Your urge to cast within the sea
Has it returned to harry thee

Such wayward dreams within the vest
Should be forever laid to rest
Let not thy kingdom's walls be probed
By choking vines, desire disrobed

Look hard my friend into my eyes
My friend who laughs, but never cries
Your stirring draws my childhood heart
Your wanton needs tear you apart

As if the whirlwind suckles you
It's how I know your lapse is due
What troubles have befallen thee
That can't between us be set free

My friend, let not your spirit fail
But by thy choosing, walk your trail
And know that if your choice is right
That you will see a better light

Life

As time rolled back the years
I slowly grew aware of this
That life must have its tears

Far from the shores of birth
Far from the days of innocence
We age upon this earth

In mortal clay we stand
Bewitched by all life gives to us
Forever plow in hand

We see what all we can
But see far less of what's ignored
Such is the sight of man

Till finally we stop
Upon this road that led uphill
To life's great mountain top

Non Fatalism

In a world of dreamers dreaming
Where longing's often cruel
It's through an eye of a needle
That success is threaded through

For the bear that we all rode on
From the day that we came in
Was a destiny that could be changed
To goals that we can win

With the pressure always mounting
To fill your heart and soul
Sometimes it takes a change in mind
For you to take control

Yet dreams will breathe for any
Who'll take the time to see
So too each moment that goes by
Just let your heart be free

There are many who will go seeking
Distractions where they may
It's how they bury their despair
In any kind of play

But in the end you'll tally
Each moment that went by
You'll either lived a rich sown life
Or didn't even try

Presently Here

Tomorrow may glitter of a new dawn
But cherish today before you move on

Whether the path is beaten or new
Keep to your stride with goals you pursue

Destiny's ring is hollow they say
When reaching beyond for the following day

The present is where our living is at
So roll up your sleeves and hang up your hat

Time will not keep us early or late
But only to share the road to our fate

The path to tomorrow is only to end
Quickly enough around the next bend

Rejection

Nothing stings harder than the strike of rejection
It's able to surpass the most formidable of walls
And lance the heart sternly of all of its passion
Tis the worse to forget, and the fall of all falls

We strive with our hearts to just be accepted
We strive with ironies that plague life itself
But deep in the core of our actual existence
Lies a need to be more in the eyes of our self

The willingness to make us completely so vulnerable
To chance beyond reason or ability to think
We place ourselves hanging on the sufferance of others
It's desire's golden mystery, to swim or to sink

We live with the need to simply be valued
We live with the need for attention and love
It is our nature to dare against dangers
That makes us so worthy in what we seek of

The tenacity expended in facing long chances
The insatiable hunger for the gem of desire
It matters not ever what the heart will seek after
Be it love, fame or fortune, the reasons catch fire

Why does it matter to act like all people
Like lemmings who follow their kin to the sea
It's in our true nature to worship our dreaming
By forestalling the brakes, letting chance to run free

The Bump in the Road

Please show to me another way
A way beyond what's given
Where none will see the ending day
At least to those still livin'

We'll see the light fade out at night
When night comes softly calling
And shed its cloak before the bite
The bite that has you falling

How can we slip that bridging gate
From one breath to another
To find that death has met its fate
No more the usher's brother

I seek Elijah's chariot
And time's swift running roan
But give me Sampson's lariat
And I'll rope eternal's throne

The Gate

It stands unfettered, without concern
Serene in its setting, simplistic and stern

So calmly content in purpose and chore
Awaiting my choice, to come or ignore

This pivotal moment of retrospect
This fork in the road that deems respect

For life would change on the choosing I make
Where the body would go, the heart too must take

I stand here before this unlocked gate
Unsure, untried, unknown to fate

And ponder long, to go or to stay
Should I open this gate, or walk away

The Priority of Reason

The leaves fall to autumn's call
Beneath a dismal gray filled sky
But only fools will brightly say
Today's a better day
The world turns without concern
To all the tears that had gone dry
Yet still an empty heart can lay
With broken dreams at may

What folly in the face of doubt
Would make a point less true
That renders some to turn about
And still chase it askew

The stars sleep in slumber deep
Without a thought for you or I
But only fools will choose to think
Their twinkle was a wink
The waves know to come and go
While luring with its gentle voice
But only will the cautious see
The dangers of the sea

What foolish choices do we make
Because of pompous pride
Will make us chase a worse mistake
Then what good sense would guide

Those Loving Hands

How much love is in those hands
Who'll help you rise when you awake
That gently aids you getting dressed
While steadies you through pain and ache

Those hands that comb your fading hair
And clean your face to greet each day
What heart could never bend or break
When helped by hands who love this way

Such are the hands who raise the spoon
To feed you with God's tenderness
How quickly they would race to you
To cleanse your lips of any mess

Those hands that spring from heaven's love
That strive to answer any plead
They care not for how long it takes
But only seek to aid your need

Just how much love is in those hands
That serve beyond each day and night
When all you have are worn out tears
As you endure, the timeless fight

Behold the hands that cradle you
And softly stroke your aging cheek
Please know that they will also pray
And bring to God what you can't speak

What Price

What price, a given smile
A simple lifting of the lips
A tenderness within the eyes
A billowing thereof the cheeks
Tis true, it is our style
When happiness took hold awhile

What price, a kindly word
A thought that rises from the heart
A breath that carries spoken love
A need to voice some worthy hope
Tis true, it's not absurd
When there's assurance to be heard

What price, a gentle touch
A stirring of a loving hand
A poignant calling from your soul
A sympathetic show of warmth
Tis true, it's known as such
When being human means this much

Words

Wilt not your heart on words that wound
Nor let it burn as tit for tat
Such ashes from a blazing heart
Someday will fill your mouth at that

Dwell not upon those callous words
Nor give them anchor to your heart
But look to see why they were broached
For thou hurt the hardest, when hurt at start

Beware the flickering, heated flame
That burns within all living souls
It looks for any given chance
To howl the beast and fan the coals

Let not your weary heart grow shallow
But keep it ever full of love
For that will thrust aside all barbs
With endless strength to rise above

Blessed are the makers of peace
And those who give, mercy to all
Let this mantra be how you live
And all the reason to stand tall

Sorrow, Despair, Regret and Loss...

A Sleepless Night

When you lie in bed at night
While in your world, things just aren't right
There're troubled waters in your mind
With answers that are hard to find
It makes you wish you'd found a way
To leave behind that day

Around and around your thoughts will screech
As sleep just lingers out of reach
A quietude pervades the air
That stirs your senses to despair
It makes you wish you'd found a way
To start another day

Your pounding heart will not slow down
The day's events go round and round
A troubled spot grows very sore
And makes your need for loving, more
Oh how you wished you'd found a way
To skip that awful day

Within the darkness of your room
With scoffing traits of any tomb
You reach across that gulf of time
And face the reason for the crime
Then reaching for the phone you say
Why wait another day

At What Point Will God Come in

Oh, how easy it must be
To run from responsibility
And see a loveless chosen world
As home to your hostility

Oh, how righteous you must feel
To shun aside all obligations
And owe not one good thought to any
By showing them considerations

Oh, what hammer you must wield
To beat aside all culpability
That lies upon your anvil heart
So you may have deniability

Oh, where has your conscience gone
And left your thoughts to fabrication
To twist all facts to please your fiction
While owing none an explanation

Oh, what price is an act of caring
Does it exceed survivability
Just where are your better angels
Who cry at your detachability

Barely

Life in a bottle, dreams in a needle
Living the good times don't come free
Running the highway, searching for someway
Finding a future for someone like me

Where are the roses, the bromide of Eden
Where are the maidens of propitious fate
Gone are the days of just feeling normal
In are the lies I use to feel great

Looking for someone, running from all
Needing no family or even a friend
Lonely and daring, willing at sharing
As long as it gets me high in the end

All of my needs are driven by hunger
Desiring a drink or a pop in the vein
Simple and scheming, and never redeeming
With despicable acts to help me maintain

Where is the ending, the cure and the mending
Where is the high to peace and success
Only from death in the shadow I'm casting
Has a solution to all of this mess

Bridges Burned

How sad it is to go this way
With no one there for you
Age has come to have its say
And solitude has too

Your life's been spent at getting free
Of those who loved you best
And now those bridges cease to be
Since laying them to rest

All dying is a frightful thing
Especially alone
But even worse than anything
The family you disown

How sad it is to have none there
To ease your suffering pain
Because you failed to see they care
Therein the past you've slain

Cry softly through your lonely night
Cry for a touching hand
Where is the love you would invite
Beyond the hearts you've banned

Broken

Will you still love me in the morning
Will you still love this broken fool
I knew I hurt you with my scorning
I knew my words were very cruel

This madness that I show is bitter
This rage I hold, I know not how
And when I see that I had hit her
I knew for us there is no now

Why isn't there a proper answer
Why isn't there a calmer sea
Why is our love so full of cancer
Why is our hate so quick to be

How long will anger run like wildfire
How long will violence rule the day
How long until the tide gets higher
And carry both of us away

Is there no heaven we can cling to
Is there no ground where peace can rule
Where are the memories that we once knew
Burned out by fire in heated duel

Why can't our love be not so broken
Why can't we face the fears we hide
Why can't we say those words unspoken
I'm sorry that we never tried

Carnal Rampage

You ripped and tore and took from me
A thing I've held so preciously
That now I live quite callously
Within the sin you brought

Roll, roll, gather no moss
A tumbling stone will feel no loss
Roll beyond the light of day
Roll beyond the guilt of prey

The sky is there for all to see
As something that's forever free
But in my eyes it'll never be
As free as what I thought

Roll, roll, gather no moss
A tumbling stone will feel no loss
Roll because you can not stay
Roll because you lost your way

No longer will a shadow be
As empty as this heart in me
But filled with dreadful memory
Of what your rape has wrought

Roll, roll, gather no moss
A tumbling stone will feel no loss
Roll forever thoughts that say
Roll forever from that day

Ever Adrift

Who will wipe your tearing eyes
Who will hear your stormy cries
And who will touch your cheek with love
Or lips to kiss your brow thereof

Is this the life, your closed heart hews
Is this the lonely road you choose
Where are the ones you disengaged
To stand beside you as you aged

Turn not your back upon your friends
Nor on your kin without amends
For life will only last one round
And love should never go to ground

It's human nature when you fall
To run away behind a wall
But try to understand this line
"To err's human, forgive's divine"

Wait not until the night draws near
Wait not until there's nothing here
But thaw the ice that caulking you
And warm the heart that I once knew

Ever adrift on stormy sea
Ever alone from family
And haunted by the demons raised
From the abyss in which you'd gazed

Goodbye

My heart is shattered all apart
My life is hardly livin'
My mind is where the dying's at
My anguish has me driven

Oh succor me from the ashes of my loving son
My loss is way too bitter
Why must the jewel of my long life
Be snatched while in the litter

I lie in harbor's stormy waters
While sorrow's ship lays anchored to my grieving heart
Torpidity's gulf enshrouds me
As my tears continue to part

It's so hard to see anyone smile
And their laughter fails to reach my ears
Yet I know that I must still carry on
While mourning for years and years

Haunted

My Jenny called me from heaven again
In a voice that was soft and pure
She whispered my name with a pleading strain
And said that our love would endure

She said that her arms are aching for me
That her lips were hungry for mine
And she needed me now, so I could see
That our love was destined to shine

Her wispy like voice, like a smoky screen
Was gripping my heart with fey
I yearned to bring her, where she could be seen
My angel of passionate sway

Oh come to me darling, come to me now
She cried and implored of me
Oh darling, it's simple, and this is how
Said my love from the Judas tree

I felt my heart flutter, missing a beat
To this desperate thought I gave
To ponder at making our love complete
By joining her there in the grave

Oh how I do miss, my sweet buttercup
Her laughter and smiling at me
I know there's no ending, or letting up
To the haunting she makes me see

My Jenny called from perdition again
In a voice of sorrow and pain
She died by hanging herself on a chain
Forever in love, and insane

The suffering she felt at her world's end
Had moved her to such a degree
That even our love wouldn't help or mend
How broken her spirit would be

Upon each and every night, I'd hear
Her haunting cries and soulless wail
It would rip at my heart, tween love and fear
So lonely the road, that I hail

How Long is too Long

How long is too long
To hold a dead child
Past the morning's new light
Past the heart's darkling cloud

To mourn without ending
To weep beyond tears
How long is too long
When each moment takes years

Where is the spirit
That once filled this life
As calm rests the body
From death's wielding knife

How long is too long
To cup your child's face
And capture each feature
Each hair in its place

To lay fevered kisses
Upon those soft cheeks
How long is too long
When seconds are weeks

Where are the angels
To wail by my side
Their crying in heaven
Can't turn back the tide

How long is too long
To clutch to your breast
The child you have given
Your heart and your best

I Use to Be

When did the world start dying
When did the sky fall down
When did my hopes go lying
Telling me, that I won't drown

Where had the up turned under
Where had the spring turned fall
Where have my dreams gone yonder
Pinning me against the wall

Why must the wind keep blowing
Why must the odds be long
Why must I keep on going
When everything goes wrong

Is life an onion season
Or a moral in a tale
Is fate sufficient reason
For the tipping of the scale

Please tell me I'm not crazy
Please tell me I'm not mad
Cause all my thoughts are hazy
When remembering is bad

I live within this bubble
Denying what I see
And stand within the rubble
Of the man I use to be

Losing Trust

Oh how cruelly our spirits were swept
By those who made promises, but ne'er were kept

How bravely our hopes had marched away
Across a dark plain, where the shattered would lay

Henceforth a struggle will rage inside
To keep disappointment, from showing outside

And as the heart is squeezed ever tight
From time's reckless pivot, prolonging the flight

It saddens our spirits to wallow and sway
To a tune that betrayal had elected to play

Trust is a fragile and vulnerable thing
It's the hardest to recover, and sharpest to sting

Lost

I felt the tears within my eyes
But drove them back, but drove them back
I'll not give in to sobs and cries
By thoughts so deeply black

My aching chest cries every day
Within my heart, within my heart
And beats so madly as it may
Intend to break apart

My wounds lie raw within my mind
So hauntingly, so hauntingly
They yearn for answers, any kind
To ease this pain in me

Each night is when it hurts the most
I want to cry, I want to cry
So lost I drift as if a ghost
Awaiting God's reply

Again the tears attempt to fall
But made them cease, but made them cease
I'll keep myself behind this wall
Where lies my only peace

My Heart in Knots

Beyond all scope of understanding
Beyond all reason known to me
I can not grasp this fact demanding
That I should know what I now see

What dire events have brought this feeling
What sadness has eclipsed your heart
I still can't fathom why you're reeling
And why you feel you must depart

Is there no other course of action
Is there no better middle ground
Am I the reason for this fraction
And why your love can not be found

No one deserves this undertaking
No one deserves such hopeless thoughts
This ending that you think of making
Has vastly tied my heart in knots

Please stop my child and reconsider
Please open up and let me in
Has life itself become so bitter
That you would want it all to end

This folly that you seek is endless
And never can be justified
So too will I forever feel this
If you're still seeking suicide

How often must I cry in sorrow
With tears that you will never see
I pray that you will see tomorrow
And all your pain has been set free

Nostalgia

There were times when I would turn around
I would look behind, and had always found
That the past was clear
With memories dear
Oh Lord, how the years unwound

I would see a face of a girl I knew
She would smile and say, are you coming too
If I knew back then
How the road would thin
So lonely, since leaving you

There's no reason why for the way I feel
I was stubborn then, and I'm stubborn still
Well I had to be
What I thought was me
Oh life, is a bitter pill

When you had no ties and were on your own
Just a kid who lived like a rolling stone
It was easy then
To be saying when
You're finally all grown

So there are times when I have a need to bow
To the ageless past which I must plow
It's a curse I trawl
That I must recall
Such times, as the time right now

Pompeii

With the consummation of ash and air
An apocalyptic voice now fills the sky
Night had woven its cape across the land
While chariots of hell, begin to fly

Oh what destruction now reigns on us
As the brimstone of Sodom and Gomorrah draws near
What chance has any to escape certain death
When the earth itself trembles, in groveling fear

Deep lies the streets in heated ash
With mounds of the near dead everywhere
Each breath inhales more soot-like flour
To cinder paste lungs, fighting for air

Despair lies thick in our darting eyes
As they roll about in uncontrollable fear
Only the dead are beyond recall
To the horror they once had suffered here

Through dark gray drifts, we struggle forth
Trying to flee what can not be fled
And any who fall will never get up
Destined to sleep in their eternal bed

Oh Pompeii, Pompeii, my cherished home
Forever the ages, you now will dwell
How quickly you passed from the realm of life
To a tomb in the shade of raging hell

Quick to Flee

Nobody ever could say why
She left each place that she had been
But when the time was right to fly
You'd knew it by her listing grin

Nothing could hold her in one place
Not even love could make her wait
She always had a dream to chase
And a watch that said, she's late

But if she ever stayed too long
Her laugh would take a lonely turn
And in her eyes there'll be no song
Just shadows of a distant burn

What made this maiden quick to flee
Before each place could hold her there
She never let her heart be free
Nor hope to linger anywhere

No wishful looks within her eyes
Nor soulful roots to stay her feet
She only hears the past that cries
Of something she can't repeat

I knew a girl I met one day
Who never paused at living life
But sunny skies turned quickly gray
When I'd asked her to be my wife

Nobody ever could say why
She left each place that she's been to
I'll only know her parting sigh
As she walked to the door and through

Randy

Oh, how long he had suffered so
Through pain no person should ever endure
The body should never be laid this low
With only the promise of even more

Oh my friend, how you made me cry
To see you hide behind laughter and smile
But way deep inside you're yearning to die
While holding to life, at least for awhile

You have gone beyond all limits of hope
And already you walk the halls of hell
Yet still you find the ability to cope
There within your mortal cell

Oh my sad friend, where are your tears
When others are crying, you laugh instead
Behind your eyes, lies the torment of years
Till finally, you embraced what you dread

Oh how now, I miss seeing you
Now that you fled from this world of vast pain
Such was the courage, in how you made do
To live without hope, was simply insane

Red Harvest Wine

When the knife falls, where will you be
Upon the lion's back, or down on your knee
When the stroke comes, how will you plea
With softly spoken voice, or roaring mightily

Red harvest time
Red harvest wine
Only blood will run
From life's grapevine

When the blade cuts, how will you feel
Moving inch by inch, moving six inch steel
When the push comes, will you reveal
Just another heart, to the killer's chill

Red harvest time
Red harvest wine
Only blood will run
At the battle line

When the knife falls, will you be free
Would you be changing, or bound helplessly
When the time comes, how will you flee
Riding on the wind, or a red harvest spree

Red harvest time
Red harvest wine
When the flask is poured
Only death will dine

Reliving the Past

Swift are the words of pain
That fly untethered and free
And to my heart it seeks its reign
Unjust, untrue, by thee

Deep was the dagger's aim
That bled my loving heart
And nevermore was life the same
Since evil played its part

All of my thoughts are gray
Leashed onto a skiving rope
And should my feelings go astray
I'll crush that ray of hope

No more will I allow
To ponder on the why of it
It hurts me far too much to plow
The past to recommit

I'll dwell not on such thoughts
Of how my world had slanted me
Less all my being twist in knots
And my mind is lost at sea

Remembering

With every beat my heart would toll
From all the anguish in my soul
My sorrow weights beyond the years
A loss that lives beyond all tears

So carry all your memories clearly
Close to that, which you hold dearly
Carry naught what makes you teary
Knowing they would want you cheery

Don't let your heart grow hard as stone
To gather moss on what you've known
But rather look at what is bright
And let it clear the dark of night

Blessed are our love ones going
Beyond the day's final showing
And blessed are the ones left mourning
Whose loss, like mine, is felt each morning

Run Through

Why have I been betrayed my Lord
Without a reason why
And cut far deeper than a sword
Beyond the need to cry

So wounded lies my broken heart
So lost in straying thought
I sit, a man so torn apart
And stare at simply naught

I can not chase this gloom away
Each dark infested night
But toss unsoundly where I lay
In repetitious plight

Where have your love receded to
Why can't the sun now shine
I never thought I'd be run through
By acts so clandestine

Hope's beyond this road I travel
Far from the mortal eye
And as I watch my world unravel
Inside, I wilt and die

Self Deception

In what world visited
Is your mind so deceived
That all of reality
Would then be perceived

By reasons outrageous
With egregious told lies
Such extravagant slander
Is contrary to wise

On what moral high ground
Are you so entrenched
That your heart has been taken
And your love has been blenched

Has your senses departed
From the judgment you use
That you cease to find question
In the thoughts that you muse

In what world so shielded
Are you bound to sustain
That your actions are poignant
By the cruelty you reign

Skeletons Were Meant to Lie

Some dark secrets are better off when put away
Lost in creases, where forever they will stay

All the time that passes by
No other voice will say
Remember all the truths that lie
Forever tucked away

In the image we construe
Like angels with pure thought
They lack the secrets that we knew
Of times when we were not

Some past moments, when resolve had lost the day
Take those dark times, and let them slip away

Behind the doors that closets hide
Are skeletons inside
They wait until a door's thrown wide
To tell of tales denied

Sometimes the story can be cruel
Which mostly is the rule
But what has passed, must stay as past
To have the future last

This Coffin

These memories that I see
These horrors I exist upon
Are all that's left of me
For nothing's left, and I am gone

Life's another shade now
In darkly halls within my heart
For guilt's to whom I now must bow
A God that won't depart

In younger days I ran
When joy was known and love would thrive
But now a haunted man
I run to stay alive

Those faces of the dead
With burning and accusing eyes
Had laid their deaths upon my bed
I have no alibis

This night that never ends
This hated coffin I'm within
Oh, how the madness rips and rends
As time repeats again

To Danger's Sudden Presence

From panic's flung hand to calm's waiting cheek, the gauntlet flew
And struck as well as any blow, was ever meant to do
Such unforeseen and suddenness had moved it tenfold more
To where the fear of dying was infallibly ashore

Race the heart unchained to the fury of the hound
Race the wind of chaos through a mind so turned around
Grim is the seeing through a sight so narrowed down
Grim is the reaper in a darkly hooded crown

What spirit so vacant could ever allow, the coward's hand
That would mark you forever, with that detestable brand
If found unbidden to death's rushing arms, how would you steer
With unflinching surety of self, or curdled by fear

Breath is the channel to life we are given
Breath is the reason to fight for our living
Breath holds the promise on which hope is driven
And has the most value, to thwart the unshriven

Transitioning

Well, well, well
It has finally reared its ugly head
The avenue of living now crosses the boulevard of death
Out are the glory days of passion and life
In are the days of great worry and strife
I am the pulse that runs down this lane
Traveling in a vehicle of earthly bane
From my Alpha beginning to my Omega end, I fare
Grasping at the reeds of atrophy
Or anything else in my anguished despair
I feel the urgency to slow it all down
Delaying, decaying, with spirit defraying
I cringe beneath God's eye
Knowing I must go, but not the reason why
Corpus is ailing and terminally failing
Christi is hailing and slowly unveiling
My salvation's at hand, but waiting within another land
Yet in this world, it's cancer's command

Unmade

So darkly deep lies the pit
The tomb to which I bed myself
And call not one to counter it
Or sweep my dusty, cloistered shelf

Cold as a lonely shoulder
That rests in a sea of lies
Hard as a fallen boulder
Is the story within my eyes

Lonely drowns all tomorrows
With passion like a hurricane
Entombed within a shell of sorrows
Where having hope is ever feign

Vast, lies this ugly feeling
That's martyred in flames of fire
Caught like a moth appearing
On the spit of its desire

I only crave dreary skies
To hide within the darkness there
My heart's been buried by all my lies
To smother me in its putrid air

Long is the hangman's shadow
Calm are the hands he field
Tight is the noose I will know
That has no room to yield

Upon the Shadow's Heel

Oh girl of cloistered keep
There within your castle walls
In woods that lie so deep

What tower holds to thee
Dark and hidden, lonely ridden
Beyond all life to see

A maiden with no smile
Whose tears will never see the sun
Thereon her heartbreak isle

No heart should walk within
The shadow of another one
As long as you have been

Let not your troubled way
Restrain you from the parting road
And from the light of day

Rejoice and let it show
Twas never meant for sorrow's sake
That heart of yours I know

Warring Love

Bold stroke sir, you have indeed
Your love, your life, you've made them bleed

While in the iron will you fey
A core of stone you would display

Rafters call your gallows name
Come they say, you are to blame

With hordes of thoughts to whip you sound
Reminding you, you're conscience bound

Oh Lord, the irony of it all
So hard I try, so hard I fall

Never will my heart be melted
Now that it's been sorely gelded

But in the realm where fates will gather
They'll mock the ones that they will feather

And goad a spark, a tease of hope
While drawing tight the hangman's rope

Cincinnatus could relate
The tug of war that is my fate

When You Lose the One You Love

Tell me how the wind keeps blowing
Tell me why the birds still sing
Is it something I'm not knowing
Since I've lost my everything

Tell me how the clouds yet tumble
Tell me why the sun still shine
Can a spirit be this humble
Since I lost this heart of mine

Has the world grown short on laughter
Has its color faded too
Will there be a morning after
To the night that came for you

Tell me how the world keeps turning
Is there anymore to give
When there's nothing left for burning
With no will to even live

Some may wonder, what's the matter
Surely I could rise above
But I say your world will shatter
When you lose the one you love

When Your World Comes Apart

What do you do when your purpose is dying
Where do you run and hide
All through the years your life's full of trying
Feeding the dreams inside
When you have seen that your visions were lying
Making you terrified
That's when you think that the time you were buying
Would help you to override

Over and over, and over again
You wrestle away from the shame
Over and over, your thoughts would spin
But it always end the same

All of your fears that you've been denying
They show whenever you cried
All of your acts were so death defying
Turning us all aside
Needless to say that the answer's not crying
Hung up on silly pride
Take all of the rules that you've been applying
And boldly throw them aside

Over and over, it's hard to begin
When you have no definite aim
Over and over, and over again
Looking for someone to blame

Over and over, you look within
Upon the road you came
And found the surface truly thin
Yet tread your thoughts the same

You Aren't Here

You aren't here to see me cry
To hold me close, to pacify

You aren't here when I am sad
When I remember what we had

For all my tears will run so free
When there is none around to see

I close up tight into a ball
At the bottom of my in-built wall

You aren't here to see my tears
The ache that stabs, the hurt that spears

You aren't here when I would shake
When all my heart begins to break

And all the pulling in I do
Will keep me safe from needing you

Within myself, within my ball
Curled up tight next to my wall

You aren't here to see my pain
When all my tears fall down like rain

You aren't here when things are bad
But all in all, I wish you had

Poetry

A Paradigm for Poetry

Upon thy hidden voice, arrive your words
That smothers all other thoughts of mine
And tumble about like frantic little birds
Determined to seek its true design

Through the mind's cerebral door, I gaze
At what had swiftly materialized
With golden meaning, now breathes a phrase
And to my poetic heart, immortalized

Such subtlety doth run the silent thought
Hidden amongst the shoal of many more
Yet piercing with power when finally caught
This offering from heaven's far shore

I focused to catch the nightingale's cry
Cutting the night, between the here and there
Forever God's herald to the moon and sky
And the poet who travels his road anywhere

This Door Upon My Lips

I say, behold this story of my waking dawn and all that
it will tell to you
And know that I had never known to speak in such a
lustful way as poets do

For none before had bared that muse like element
which brings to life, the life within
Then from this fair and lovely dove whose heart but
once had touched and healed where mine had been

It is as if you are the key from which this door upon
my lips is opened wide
Whereby such golden treasures rush to brace the
heart of whom they yearn to be their guide

This door that I had ever been so blind to know, or
even of its hidden gold
Had lain away so surely kept within the dark, as well
as dark could ever hold

It is for you and you alone, whereby my lips will usher
forth in fervid deed
Such poems that ooze poetically, with roots that can
be only found from heaven's mead

Love and Hope...

5th Avenue

Your mind has seen another way, a path you never knew
Fresh thoughts and feelings shower you, with brand new ideas too

And in that midst of mental storm, you find another need
For physical affection with an ever growing speed

The barriers that fenced your life and kept you in the game
Are finally thrown down at last and buried without shame

While all the dreams and wishes that you foster or construe
Of happiness, good fun and love, you'd found they do come true

So when the sun comes up again to fill your world with light
Just think of all the joy ahead, and life shall be more bright

As changes come into our lives and put us to the test
Through pain, worry and despair, we'll lay our doubts to rest

And step to meet the future, with all our very best

Again

There's sunshine in your perfect eyes that dance in pure delight
A sparkling and heartfelt surprise, I revel in their sight

For when you smile it touches me, and last forever after
So too it is like music when I hear your healing laughter

I feel so whole when you are here, a part of me I missed
Yet shake with need to hold you near, I'll faint should I be kissed

But if I earned no other boon than just to touch your hair
My chest would pop from burning fires that raged inside of there

So save my days and nights my love, by throwing down the pin
And spare this bubble that I'm on, by seeing me again

Ancient Wisdom

I love when you would hold me tight and whisper of
"How wonderful it feels to have this growing love"

Then I would say quite softly near your darling ears
"I'm here to stay so put behind your darkest fears"

Yet in your eyes I see a need, a pleading cry
"Please care for me forever love until we die"

Then gently I would kiss your lips and say to you
"I'll always make you happy, this you know is true"

While in their chatter, chirping clatter, birds would say
"She's such a pretty flower in just every way"

And as the winds blow soothingly across her sky
They'll whistle through her lovely hair a happy sigh

So if the earth, the moon, and all the sky can hold you dear
Then by their ancient wisdom I will too adhere
By showing all my love to you, each passing year

And Destined Ne'er to be Apart

Take hold of your quarrel my love
The bolt you spent to fickle me
And gently take thy shaft in hand
While pressing home your lips gently

Yea taketh back that deadly sting
That Cupid gave you leave to free
For it is far too much to bare
This love of mine, now twice to be

There wasn't need for this, your ply
For I was yours before the let
But with your arrow now in heart
My love doth rage its martinet

Beware my love, my hunger now
For it must feast on all of you
And all of you will feel my flame
Whose wick's been turned a brighter hue

Is it not so my sacred dove
Is it not so within thy heart
We both are tangled by our lures
And destined ne'er to be apart

As We Would Nestle In

Within the depths of any night
The feeling's right, the heart is bright
It makes us want to cling real tight
As we would nestle in

And when the cold would show its might
A chilling bite, but only slight
Because we'd always took delight
As we would nestle in

She'll snuggle up real close to me
So happily, and cheerfully
Her heart would beat so pleasingly
Within my reaching arms

She's such a pretty girl to see
So verily, you would agree
And all her love goes eagerly
Within my reaching arms

Our time would have another rate
To consummate, and punctuate
Whenever we would make a date
To show our growing love

And even if the night is late
We never wait, or hesitate
No matter what life has in fate
We'll show our growing love

Closest One

What a day it is for me my friend
What a day it is to see my friend
All the joys and happiness that you bring
Oh my friend, you're like the spring

In the time I've spent with you my friend
In the pleasures that we do my friend
I could never say that it wasn't true
These feelings I have for you

Dawn's always in my sky my friend
On a note that makes me cry my friend
I've never been so alive my friend
Since the day that I met you

Fever

What fever burns me so
And drives the swallow from my mouth
By fires from way down low

This heat which can be seen
As twitching here and twitching there
And twitching in between

Has all my breath expired
Constricted by this base desire
To purge my loins so wired

Is this some form of drug
Where all my will has slipped away
Or Lilith's meddling tug

Am I the fool to think
That love is just a passive thing
And wine a simple drink

What heart would not be awed
And stumble not, each beat by beat
When love itself has called

Find the Way to Love

Emptiness is dealing with a deep down lonely feeling
And the only way for healing is to find the way to love
It's endless plains of yearning where the dust is often churning
From the storms within us burning for this need that I speak of

Heaven is truly just a corner away
Where laughter rings golden, day after day
And sunny means more than the sky overhead
It's all the good cheer that you bring instead

Walls are hard at hearing when your voice is often clearing
Of the sobs which have you nearing to a final breaking down
Often we are fleeing from the figure that we're seeing
Of a lonely heart spent being in the mirror that we crown

Open the doors to the smiles you kept inside
Show the world all those treasures that you hide
Let no limits be the end to what you do
But just beginnings to the goals that you pursue

First Love

What can a bird do, beyond its sheltered nest
Or a baby bear waking, from its long winter's rest

Such are the young living their life
Where first love finds even more
A purity where the heart would soar

How can the geese fly, in lines so straight and true
Or baby ducks who waddle by, in such a perfect queue

Such are the young with all their heart
Where first love in its endless might
Burns brighter than any light

What rose richly scented, could escape any bee
Or the scent of the ocean, from a wind blowing free

Such are the young in their first love
Whose passion knows no mortal measure
But plunders hard life's solemn treasure

Forever Yours

If the wind, swept the blue
From the heart of the sky
And blew the stars askew
From the beds where they lie

Yet still my heart would claim to be
Forever yours eternally

If the seas ran away
From the shores of the land
And left the beaches fey
Without waves to command

Yet still my love would always be
Forever yours eternally

And if time should abate
To the vessels we prize
By a hitch to our gait
And a crease to our eyes

Yet still my thoughts would cling to thee
For all of eternity

Going All the Way

Cinnamon lips, I surely would miss
A chance at collecting a passionate kiss

Peaches for cheeks, there's never been such
Beg for my fingers in tenderly touch

Bright starry eyes have flooded my night
With glittering colors of love's awesome might

Strands of pure honey would wave everywhere
As the wind takes pleasure in catching her hair

I'll lose all composure, my heart would go still
Whenever she'd beckoned for me to her will

Then like a soft flower, her voice would unfold
To capture my heart in a magical hold

So sweet is the sound of her spoken name
My Donna has caught me in love's burning flame

No matter how far we'll go on life's ride
Forever we'll travel by each other's side

Growing in our Garden

You are no desert flower, where life is scarce and dry
You thrive on warmth and sunshine, far from the desert sky

Most flowers of the desert, they often live alone
Their roots get little substance amidst the desert stone

While only cactus flowers can live without much rain
They hide behind their needles, their hollow lives are plain

But you're not of the desert, there's much that you care of
You're tender and you're vulnerable, with feelings full of love

So I beg for your dear pardon, please come and grow with me
We both are lonely flowers with a need for company

It's a shame we're only flowers, when a man I'd rather be
But there's more than vegetating, there are dreams that need set free

So if you would be my woman, as I would be your man
You'd find us growing closer than what lonely flowers can

Lift High Your Hair

Short was the day, and long is the night
And even though my soul takes flight
My love for you will always fare
Whatever course that I must bare

Let not the sadness steal all thought
Nor swell your eyes with tears you swat
But think the happy, good thoughts of me
And how our journey had harmony

Waste not your heart on pageant woes
Nor of your time in wistful pose
But let the wind lift high your hair
And dance that dance that we had there

Live, sing, show the world your smile
You'll see me in another mile
Although your road has more to see
Enjoy each day, with love, from me

Locked in Love

Each time I feel her touch on me
Her warm embrace
Her smiling face
My heart would race
And all because I'm holding thee

With naked skin so smooth and fair
Your eyes will glow
And seek to show
The love you know
I bask within the love you share

Oh how I rush to have your kiss
Each time I do
My lips on you
I feel so new
There is no finer joy than this

My home is in the arms of thee
With open heart
Right from the start
I'll never part
I'm locked in love without a key

Longing for the Evermore

Softly touching, heartbeat rushing
Longing for the evermore
Feeling, willing, hearts revealing
Love has filled us to the core

Morning laughter, shortly after
Night pans out before sunrise
Pools of merry, I find very
Often stirring in her eyes

Glowing, knowing, that it's showing
All my happiness is true
Burning brightly, holding tightly
To the fire I have for you

Let no salt find wounds of fault
To chase away our love held dear
And may the reckless find no nexus
To the words our tongues would steer

The earth will shift as clouds would drift
By pressures from the land and sea
But only love can stay thereof
With steadiness for all to see

Along the shores of our tomorrow
Our destiny will strike the band
Be it here or past the river
We'll go dancing hand in hand

Love Is

What joy I find within a hug
Of loving arms that shelter me
Such is the peace of feeling snug
In knowing that it's meant to be

Love is an earthly song
That's been here from the start
To all the ages it plays strong
And fully to the heart

Whose breath destroyed by one true kiss
Could ever then draw breath again
Such is the warmth of savage bliss
When your soft lips had pulled me in

Love is a fatal sting
That can't be turned aside
For Cupid's arrow must take wing
To shift your world inside

What pause in time must I endure
When I would gaze into your eyes
Forever will that moment soar
Therein the midst of your sunrise

Love is a golden tear
That fell from heaven's sky
To rain upon our mortal sphere
The hearts of you and I

Morning Call

Wake up darling, it's time to rise
And let the sunshine open your eyes
Oh how the bluebird's call is dear
Tweet, tweet-tweet in my ear

Wake up my darling, the day is new
And smell the morning's fresh scented dew
Oh how the flowers grace the air
With a love we both can share

Wake up my darling, and don't be long
Hear all the church bells singing their song
Oh how they ring so pure and true
Ding, ding-dong, awaking you

Wake up my darling and look at me
And see the loving I have for thee
Oh how my arms do ache to hold
My precious darling of gold

My Every Night

She has the stars within her grasp
They'll twinkle to her smile
On any night you'll hear them gasp
If she is out that night
The stars will shine more bright

And as I walk the moon will beam
To light my going way
It'll give more substance to my dream
Of always holding her
Love's cauldron is astir

I feel love's fingers on my heart
That tightens more and more
It only seeks to play its part
No matter night or day
I pray she'll come my way

So with a lusty breath that's drawn
I'll walk the path she's on
Then hope the chance to meet will dawn
By trusting it was fate
That love would never wait

My Flower

You are my morning flower
And all my heart's desire
Your fragrance has a power
That sets my loins on fire

Your blossomy perfection
Has captured all my mind
And built a stout erection
Of love that's hard to find

Each day I seek to ravish
Some nectar from your lips
Sweet kisses that you lavish
Sweet kisses from your hips

Your heart has my devotion
Your flesh I'll wine and dine
I need no sacred potion
To have you always mine

My Quenchless Craving

Enchanted by your beauty
Yet all my vision's been eclipsed
By breasts so ample
Begging for my kisses
But drawn with fervor to your lips

All reason has departed
Bled away by Cupid's arrow
Lodged within my heart
Beating out its passion
And chasing off the maiden's sparrow

Such fire erupts my loins
As I would quake to thoughts of you
My looking and my longing
Fills me with a hunger
And sets ablaze my lust for you

My dear, dewy delight
I lurch in all my anguished need
Bare your sheltered roses
Dripping rich in nectar
And mount your gallant steed

Our Legend of Love

If I should hold to memories
I'd only find that they would tease
I'd rather have the present please
Of holding onto you

Within the light of any star
It doesn't matter if it's far
It still would shine on what you are
The prettiest girl I knew

The power of your inner grace
I see upon your loving face
You make me fit right into place
Together there with you

Upon this bubble that we top
I never want to see it pop
My love for you will never stop
As long as we are true

Our Walk

Spring's long over and summer's passed
And now our autumn days are massed

These years have come and gone so quick
With memories lying deep and thick

Yet still I find heaven's sweet isle
Each time you grace me with your smile

For happiness surpassed our tears
And brought us to our Golden years

No sound of horns or marching band
Just you and I, with hand in hand

And when life's winter touch our skies
Our love will warm us through our eyes

Till final breath has come and gone
And called us to another dawn

Still Fresh

I can't help but get excited
Every time my babe's delighted
Over something that I said or did for her

How her eyes would sparkle brightly
And her arms would hold me tightly
With a magic that our love could only stir

In the beacon of her laughter
Like a lighthouse to guide after
It will ease me past those straits along the way

I can't help but feel completed
Every time that I am greeted
When I'm gone for just a minute or all day

All my life I've had this feeling
With my tears that yearn for spilling
Was a heartache that had only grew and grew

It had changed when I selected
This fine girl whom I've detected
Who had opened up my heart and made me new

And now I'm loving every day I have with you

Stolid in Stone Hearts

Have you not eyes to behold me
Then look upon my sodden face
Know not how precious are my tears
Which you had deemed to not embrace

Where are thy strong and loving arms
Are they so filled with lead, yet still
Do you not know the might they have
That in your grasp, I'm at your will

Shun not your lips from kissing mine
Nor turn your face to face away
I have not armor to endure
The wounds I get in this cruel way

Why have you stilled your willful tongue
To wrest from me your golden voice
Let not my ears betray my trust
As silence as your wrathful choice

Has Cupid's arrow fallen yonder
Beyond the cockles of your heart
Smitten, I lie upon your doorstep
Awaiting for the veils to part

So do not fare upon this folly
By brushing aside Rhoecus' bee
Your thoughts can not be always quiet
Knowing of my love for thee

The Bastion of Myself

Oh sharp tongue of thee
No sword has thy edge
You'll cut to the quick of me
Despite our sacred pledge

Ages have tempered well
Your skill at such flaying
And upon the songs you sell
Is the rasp of hounds baying

To flee is like still water
In the face of rushing flood
Our steam gets only hotter
With the rise of boiling blood

So weak and battered am I
In the trenches of my heart
It's where my last defense will lie
And where the end will start

Against ranks of scorn and hate
That scurry up my slopes
Yet still I guard the final gate
That houses all my hopes

So come and take your measure
As I weakly wait thereof
Either way, you'll have my treasure
The laurels of my love

The Good Hurt

That lover's ache, that smitten pain
Such is the good hurt, in love's domain
When life acquires its many shades
It's love whose color, never fades

That yearning tug, that endless sting
Will drown all needs, but this one thing
For love has grasped the beating heart
And whisked our senses all apart

For who has not been disemboweled
On heavens thorn, its love unplowed
Tis one and all upon this earth
Beholden to this gift of worth

That luring draw, that potent charge
That drives us forth in Cupid's smarge
And when the bells of heaven ring
Another heart has found the spring

That golden light, that's sharply crisp
Is not the sprite, called Will the Wisp
But it is something better though
And that which never, cease to glow

The Thread of Love

Just look deep within ourselves
Past the flesh, past the bone
Whenever there are doubts of us
And all the love we've known

Search until you find that thread
Tied to me, tied to you
Anchored to our hearts we said
We'll let our love be true

Upon that thread we've added on
Over, under, and around
Fiber that we've surely won
From love that we have found

Now you've learned this precious thing
Has progressed, and been blessed
Grew from thread into a string
The bond has coalesced

Spinning fast, it grew and grew
String to twine, twine to cord
Stronger, tighter, then we knew
While in our hearts it roared

Sturdy rope now greets the eye
Very strong, very stout
Hardened by the years passed by
Erasing any doubt

Finally we looked beyond
Seeing you, seeing me
We feel the strength of our bond
This love will always be

And now our love's a sturdy rope
Tempered by our heart's desire
Firmly lies our future scope
Beyond the scathe of fire

Time is Forever, When I'm in Your Eyes

I've seen the sun shine through your eyes
With ever the morning's dawn within
It pierces me with voiceless cries
To never let this moment end

Such timeless treasured moment here
When caught within your gaze, I feel
Forever will this truth ring clear
That love's eternal bliss is real

Hold high the lantern called your heart
To light the path that I would take
Through guiding rays of love I'll start
The pilgrimage my love will make

Waiting on You

In the subdued hours on a clear summer day
As the wind whispers softly through a field of hay
And the gold of the earth met the blue of the sky
How lazy am I

Where the cedars sway so silent with ease
In a land that only has the sun and the breeze
What tales could be offered by those passing by
How lazy am I

And sitting there basking in the sun, in a row
Upon an old broken fence near an old scarecrow
Were several little birds who could verify
How lazy am I

While clouds drift leisurely in an ocean of blue
Above a grassy knoll where I wait for you
And I wondered if they could see from the sky
How lazy am I

So I patiently wait in that glorious land
For the moment when time brings you back to my hand
Then you'll smile as you say with a gleam in your eye
How lazy am I

What Voice But Mine

What pleading voice would not revert
And turn back in upon itself
To choke in fitful, longing sobs
In yearning for dear Cupid's wealth

What voice would dare take leave to try
To challenge chance, while chancing may
Succumb to growing anxiousness
And wail in stuttering disarray

What voice could say such fitting words
To shower thus thy perfect flame
Yet dousing not thy ardent fire
While dodging past eternal shame

What voice could lull your ears to sleep
Thus reaching then your treasured heart
To win forever of thy love
And of a life to never part

What voice but mine, did journey forth
To wrest from thee thy endless love
That laid forever in safe keep
From all who sought before thereof

What World Are You

What world knows not of love
Nor of its luring call thereof
And felt not once its touch
Nor called it by its name as such

What world would drinketh naught
When Cupid's cup is raised for draught
Such is the world's true need
To drink the fare that hearts would bleed

What world would not trust love
For isn't love worth trusting of
When love would give the same
To any world it's sacred flame

Sing forth, oh nature's choir
Your voices do not lack desire
And speed our worldly lot
By strengthening the love we plot

And so I say to thee
What world do you so claim to be
Beyond the breath of love
Beyond what all are fashioned of

Will Come Again No More

The ship that I've been sailing on
Before I landed here
Had taken me through stormy seas
And through each loveless year

When time had reached redundancy
I saw a true sunrise
Which only angels could compare
With dawn within their eyes

I'd never thought that I would find
A shore beyond the seas
My struggles seemed so long and hard
With nights so chafed with pleas

But there unto the east I saw
Upon the blue horizon
A golden star that caught my heart
Within your eyes arising

So now that I had found this day
I'm sailing with great speed
It's time for me to put ashore
And time my love be freed

I'll only ask that what we build
Will stay forever free
For none should own the hearts we have
Controlling you and me

So open up your loving arms
This harbor I steer for
And tell me that my sailing days
Will come again no more

You Are Here and So Am I

Baby darling don't you know that you are here
Come inside from all the pain and all the fear
That you had kept hidden
Year by year, year by year

Let me show you what my love can really do
Let me take you to a world where love is true
Where happiness is me
Pleasing you, pleasing you

Baby darling don't you know you needn't pay
Good times aren't as real when you get it this way
Just let the sun shine through
Day by day, day by day

A time will come when all the dark will pass you by
Then you'll know that when you live, it's not a lie
So let it out and so will I
You and I, you and I

You

Never a moment to pass me by
Never a thought to wander
Always in need to hold you by
Adrift in time we wander

Morning to night I think of you
Always our lips entwine
Morning to night I cling to you
With love as sweet as wine

You opened my heart, my eyes, and soul
You opened my arms to you
Forever is our spoken goal
Forever I'll love you

Vanity...

In Search of Yeats

Footsore I be, but never tired
While purpose sings to what's desired
Yea, let all the stones beware my treading
And all my roads, to be dreading
For I do come to thee

Although the wind will laugh near hie
By what a stomach could imply
Yet all my strength had proper feeding
But of the wind, its mirth is bleeding
For I do come to thee

Should time disclose to me her sweat
To sting my eyes from years I whet
Then I shall go beyond its gleaning
To such a road of ageless meaning
Then I will be with thee

Misdirection

Long have I chased the shadows of my dreams
And did not truly come to see
For if I had just turned about
I'd find my shadow chasing me

Long have I stood upon my mountain
And raised my voice for all to hear
Did I so yearn to hear my echo
That nothing else had reached my ear

And thus it was that in my longing
To find the spring that fills all hearts
That I would miss how love was flowing
While more entranced with how it starts

My Gesture

Such romantic fodder I've become
To rise before their gunning eyes
Then plummet like a plum

Oh, to just suppress my heart's desire
That, which conjures beyond the pen
They'll burn me in such critique's fire

Although it's time that shall proclaim
And bring to light so all can see
Of that, which is, will be in name

Vanity

Is it vanity to want the stars
To be the hero, to be the light
And ever burn the wick of time
Yearning to shine long past the night

Is it vanity to want their hearts
To woo their tears, to make them thirst
And I the rod that brings it down
The lightening of a poets verse

Is it vanity to want to fly
To paint the heavens, to spoon the air
And cast a shadow far and wide
Where eternal hearts will fare

Oh vanity, my vanity
I languish upon thy coals
And suffer through thy fluting sounds
That lures the hungry souls

War...

A Cry in Kuwait

What cause has thee belabored on
To make thy will so captured by
That from one prick of Satan's thorn
Such eagerness could fill your eye

What tale could I bewail for you
To fill thy gluttonous, hungry ears
With all the breath my soul could spew
So you can justify my fears

What harbor could I hide within
That would withstand thy vicious blows
With hope that when you strike again
My pain would fade as death arose

Thy hate has grown into a love
Where such ungodly acts are freed
To stroke the flesh with Nero's glove
And drop by drop my blood to bleed

What right has thee to thus attack
And pilferage our country dry
Have all the masses of Iraq
Succumbed to Saddam's evil lie

Consumption

Oh brother, brother
Where is your smile
Left behind so many a mile

When you set forth you had it then
I long to see it once again
But in your eyes you're over there
So lost, so sad, still in despair

Oh brother, brother
You're here, not there
You're not where bombs fall everywhere

Your voice grows weaker day by day
And you would have much less to say
I try my best to waken you
Into this world that you once knew

Oh brother, brother
I curse the luck that sent you from
Our loving home to Vietnam

Dear Diary

They came today to our street
And broke down our neighbor's door
I felt my rising heartbeat
As I watched them from our floor

They dragged our neighbors outside
Then beat them near to death
Oh how their children had cried
And severed all my breath

They shot the father right there
Then shot the mother too
Such is the price when you dare
To harbor any Jew

I could not watch this longer
But I could not turn away
The horror just gets stronger
As we face each dreadful day

How long must we stay hiding
In this attic full of gloom
That leaves me just confiding
To this journal I consume

Dear diary, I write only
As a girl who's named Anne Frank
Whose life is ever lonely
But alive, with much to thank

Forever There

The eye of death is upon us
We who lost our fear of dying
Somewhere amidst the battles
Amidst the endless crying

Each sunrise is an agony
For us to move ahead
While sunsets are a natural way
Of shutting out the dead

So easily it's been proven
How death can thus be sown
My hands reflect my soulful shame
To a music of their own

The wind will whisper chillingly
So mercilessly to all
And those who feel its breezy breath
Of death, will rue its squall

So inured by what we're doing
Our humanity would stop
And when the battle passes on
We have no mental prop

Thus in the end there's beauty
In the lure to die someday
It's hard to have a valid life
When everyday you pay

Home Again

I look down at the bloody mud that lies upon the ground
And would pretend I was alone with no one else around
A tender sounding lullaby keeps playing in my mind
Its music soothes my troubled heart and leaves this war behind

For just a little moment, my peace is near complete
As I lean against the trench's wall, staring at my feet
The music takes me back in time unto another place
It takes me where I'm home again, in mother's warm embrace

Oh take me home where I belong
Oh take me home sweet childhood song
Oh take me far from all of this
This dark and deep abyss

Voices try to shout away the memories that I'd freed
They only want for me to feel the pain that soldiers heed
I push myself so very hard to not hear what they say
And while my lullaby still plays, I am not here today

Yet still I feel the shaking ground as battered dirt returned
It rains upon my covered head and on the earth it spurned
I feel it slipping fast away, my home and childhood song
As once again I find myself where death and I belong

Oh mama, I am trying hard
Here in the devil's graveyard
Oh mama, you are what I miss
Beyond this dark abyss

I felt my tears slip down my cheeks and land upon my feet
As blurry vision clouded all, I hear the whistle's tweet
That was the signal for us boys to climb the muddy wall
And move against the enemy with hopes we wouldn't fall

No longer was my lullaby parading in my head
For home was gone and I've returned, and soon to join the dead
My hands now shake as I climbed out, on legs that wouldn't run
But moved more with a shuffling, as the other lads had done

Help me, my thoughts were teeming
Help me, the boys were screaming
Help me, my voice could not cry this
Within the dark abyss

If I could only turn back time and see my folks again
I'd tell them things that I held back, for I was proud and vain
Such insights that I once believed, of winning this damn war
Were just a child's imagination, to think I could do more

And so I lurched my way ahead, ignoring what I see
I do not want to freak all out, when seeing death's debris
The twisted, mangled bodies of my fellow countrymen
Are strewn about in parts and pieces, here in the damned Ardennes

Come back to me sweet lullaby
Come take me home, I cry
Oh mama, help me live through this
Deep in the dark abyss

How Sweet It Is

It'd be a shame if we were lacking
This fellowship of war
Such niceties as hacking
At each other by the score

That sweet despotic feeling
That fills us with such ease
Is deeply so appealing
To be doing as we please

For battle has its pleasure
And the winning's pure delight
In war there is no measure
In how dirty you can fight

Yes, I love that rush of madness
When scalping goes real great
There's nothing like the hard press
When you're bayoneting straight

So if your son or daughter
Have a thirst for something more
Then seek my school of slaughter
Where I'll fill their cups with war

My Memorial Day

I've traveled the way of banners
In fields devoid of life
I've seen the chosen harvest
Awaiting for the knife

I've walked on trails of glory
Where angels had been crying
Their weeping's for the harvest
For those among the dying

I've heeded to my duty
Esteemed a deadly one
But wasn't to be taken
When the harvest had begun

If I could walk those trails
The ones I had before
I'd resurrect some flowers
That had felt the sting of war

I know that it is futile
To dwell unendingly
But often I am crying
Why them, and why not me

So in the eyes of heaven
I pray that they are there
They'll see this weathered flower
And know that I still care

Salute

One if by Land

What foe are they that we march to
No hurried pace or routing chase
Just steady walking, straight and true

While across the hollow taking aim
The orifice of heavens bounds
Make ready for its earthly claim

My brow did sweat and take a toll
As beads of fear ran down my face
Yet still our pace was just a stroll

By all my given years I own
No other charge was brought this close
Where details of the foe lay known

And still we marched so ever slow
While asking of, ourselves in thought
Are we to fight, or woo this foe

Then as their muskets touched their brows
It was just then that I perceived
Upon their faces, wolfish smiles

My heart did hammer out its bleat
And knew it then, what fate gave us
That we had marched to sure defeat

It was as if we all concurred
Upon this tragic course we fared
For from our lips our moans were heard

Thus did our foolish keening break
Such spells if any, were on them
And from their guns, a hell did wake

Small clouds of bluish smoke arose
As newly ones so quickly trailed
While all we offered were our throes

It was to be an easy charge
Against a rabble, heartless few
Instead we met a foe quite large

Oh how we suffered much that day
From how our leaders sorely erred
To strut us forth in daunting way

We didn't help our cause too well
But only served to give them heart
And fight much harder 'gainst our swell

My ears still don their rally cry
That they throughout this fight would use
A sting that we were forced to ply

Back to back with words held holy
They chaffed our ears with what they cried
"Remember brothers, dear Paoli"

To me there is an inner place
That braces up my earthly plume
But touches not this world we brace

I speak of that which we do call
The fortress that our angels keep
And that which on this day did fall

For hell did rise and claimed this day
To overlap this hollow here
With thirsting men intent to slay

My God, I don't know why I live
Unscathed by all that happened here
But know, my thanks, I'll always give

For if I could, I'd keep our way
From ever touching hell again
And ever bringing short the day

I say let hell and heaven lie
Beyond this footstep we live on
Until a natural time to die

Our War Like Way

Within the woods we tarry
Our arms are all we carry
With stealthy grace, we marched our pace
While all our eyes are wary

In early morning silence
With thoughts of warring violence
We wondered all, if death would call
Our souls into her guidance

Then from our forest haven
The plains we now go braving
We trample wheat beneath our feet
And cared not for its saving

In speed we trust our keeping
To catch the foe still sleeping
The hardest part, is keeping heart
And not let fear to deepen

Then out of the sun we're streaming
Our swords and shields a gleaming
We dealt the foe an awesome blow
And filled the sky with screaming

So White the Snow

So white the snow, so dark the skies
So dense with fear in all our eyes
And soon the drums are hard at play
Commanding us away

So crisp the snow, so slow we walk
So quiet with no need to talk
For all of us were deep in thought
That hell would soon be wrought

So dry our throats, so steamed our breath
So near in time to certain death
For soon the angels high will cry
When men begin to die

Then came a roaring crackling sound
As guns ripped earth and flesh around
And in that moment God was found
With pleas sent heaven bound

So red the snow, so wet the skies
As drops of blood sprayed in our eyes
Yet still the drums were hard at play
Commanding us to stay

St. Crispin's Day

I know not why that I should lapse in spirit here before
this charging spartan tide
When all my past has driven me with eagerness to be
where I now wait to ride

Oh death does pound upon the morning's air, from all
the hoofs of horses striking ground
And I do know, that through this fog does race the
blood of many soon to flow abound

What essence bathes my open mouth, so filled with
cotton that my throat would stick in pain
Is it the taste of fear I tongue, which vastly chokes all
other senses that remain

While in my hand, my sword grows more than what its
weight should really be just moments past
That draws a cry within my mind of pure distress, and
to the heavens I now cast

Oh Lord, let all the world see here today this fight of
fights proceed as it was justly planned
And do take pity on this man who reeks with doubt
and smells of fear, to make a stand

For on this day as well as past, we did the work our
king has justly shown we must
But never had we faced such odds as those we now
must battle with, with only trust

Thus looking left and right did show that I was not
alone in all my quaking fright
For there within my fellow knights I saw the terror in
their eyes unfold with might

Yet through it all, our waiting did so bring about
acceptance of our cornered fate
Thus in this knowledge we then found a stern resolve
which also lit our eyes with weight

Our king then cried and bid us all to take to arms and
faultlessly be sound of mind
That what we do, we do in justly righteousness from
which our God would truly bind

I know that right is on our side, yet there before awaits
the fog to be estranged
And thus give way to warring forces, piercing it, as if it
could be rearranged

Oh hear those mighty horses thunder, pounding hard
the earth as if they were in hell
Bent upon the deed of flying, before the wind, and like
a ram in heated swell

Run my judgment tells me, but I will not turn tail, less
all my senses leave me
For even now I'm fading, fast away from fear, and calm
before the raging sea

Come and taste our iron, be it of our heart or of our
cherished homeland soil
And rest thee now good men, foe to English cousins,
here within your land so loyal

For had you known whereby today, this outcome was
divined and predetermined so
Then all of France would surely save this virgin field of
Agincourt, a smirching blow

But who's to say the past is past until the deed has
come to pass, before time's say
So let's fulfill our mark in time, and have all futures
thus recall, St. Crispin's Day

Sunset

With only a parting sob and a gulp that cried despair
My liquid filmed eyes gazed longingly, to sea in silent prayer

As the very last ship raced furiously, away from the dark of men
It left behind the horror of war, and the death of my Phnom Penh

So numbed with the fear of dying, my ears were sadly horrified
To hear the endless crying from all of those so terrified

We waited for their arrival, in evil subterfuge
Those killers of life, killers of love, Satan's Khmer Rouge

The Passage of William Owen

(Soldier and Poet of WWI)

My eyes belong to God
And all that passes here before
Upon this road I trod

We see each day unfold
For time will march them one by one
With all that they behold

So thus revealed this day
No more or less than those before
That harkens me to pray

Then praying, I begin
My voice beseeches God to see
This troubled land I'm in

Discern the dark gray mud
Forever stained and torn apart
And streaked with all our blood

Behold the wretched smell
That festers like a sticky gel
And called, the taste of hell

Oh hear those wounded cries
That gurgle like a summer's brook
A sound that shreds the skies

Do witness what is here
The shattered and the soon to be
Beneath this sea of fear

I've only one true thought
That God will see my suffering
And save me from this lot

War's Tempest Past

Oh my sonny, dearest love, lost and last
Your smile beckons for me within
Comforting the father that was of past
While never knowing where I had been

Love's grave lies shallow within my heart
And you alone stand forth before it
Keeping me and the living death apart
As I turn and turn upon hell's spit

Oh the ravages that whore has brought
She plunged me deep into her horror
To milk the blood of others caught
While chaining me in timeless sorrow

Oh my ageless boy, your picture's more than gold
The years have passed you by so well
As daily I will gently hold
This long past vision words can't tell

If you only knew my endless plight
And how the whirlwind calls my name
It plunges all my thoughts to night
And all my senses to the flame

When Thunder's Roll Returned

Rising well before the sunrise and off to do our chore
We climbed into our saddles on our faithful steeds once more

Their neighing was a welcome as they tossed their heads about
With an eagerness they brandished to be up and ridden out

Then through the open gateway to a land that nature blessed
We took to measured silence with a pace that's hardly pressed

Our horses slowly galloped with the stars still in the sky
With steamy breath diffusing just as quick as we rode by

And so the miles were leisurely subdued along our way
That finally brought forth the dawn, and glory of the day

With the sun so sharply rising, all our spirits too replied
Through the hills, valleys, fields and streams, such beauty was our
guide

All the birds were sweetly calling from a green and leafy sea
It appeared that Mother Nature had produced a reverie

For upon this morning venture, the pendulum had turned
And the destinies of many souls would very soon be learned

We have always sat in ambush for the foe each passing day
Twas the lives of many soldiers we have taken in this way

But as we rode in silence on majestic steeds of war
It became our turn in ambush, as they evened up the score

Religion...

A Saint's Darkest Hour

Behold the twisted body
Whose hands clench openly in taunt position
Desiring to be like claws
While acquiring strength through evil transition

The room writhes about with fear
Like a cloud of darkness seeking out all light
Causing God's words to buckle
As they relentlessly pummel evil's might

God's words come, and can be seen
True and blessed, as sacred words of holy power
That infallibly deepens
His will in this exorcist's darkest hour

Oh see how the mouth convulses
As the white foamy eyes become more stressed
So determined to reign in life
Through the death of the innocent so possessed

Praise be God's glorious love
That unerringly guides his bound servants here
To cast out Satan's brethren
From the mortal realm that our lives must adhere

Abraham

What sacrifice could not be asked and sought by thee
What test could show no better way, then what must be

Such magnitude which hinges on my choosing way
Will show if man is worthy of your love each day

While here before me lies my offered fondest son
Who waits upon my growing nerve, and death to come

Oh dearest Isaac, may you pass in shameless peace
And know that all my guilt will never end or cease

So deeply grieves this father's heart of endless love
Yet knowing that I'll give it all to him above

My God, you'll have my praises and this deed of me
And now with poising knife I vow, "The Lord will see"

Ask God

My God, my merciful God
Reach forth and take my hand
My flesh and soul are nearly
Succumbed by sin's command

Lord Jesus, release me now
Come forth into my heart
Take hold of all my sinning
Demanding it to part

Oh Spirit, sweet Holy Spirit
Fulfill my hungry need
Let my soul behold your touch
Your presence as my mead

Hail Trinity, how great art thou
As one, your reign's complete
Bless me in this life I live
Till heaven's call to meet

Tread softly, with careful step
Lest both your feet would stray
For everywhere we walk, is sin
Ask God to lead the way

Birds of Brown

Little Jesus played
By a country stream
Happy in the glade
Angels watched him dream
Holding in his hands
Tiny bits of mud
Voicing his commands
Telling it to bud
Slowly life appeared
From his whispered word
To the sky it reared
A brown tiny bird
Happy was its cry
As Jesus let it go
Joining in the sky
Other birds in tow
All above his head
In their joyful flight
Flew these birds instead
Wouldn't leave his sight
Happy Jesus played
With his birds of brown
All of them were made
From the mud he found

By God's Grace

I have no shield before me
That can withstand thy blow
And all the armor in me
Is vanity I show

I have no magic that can
Suppress thy reaching hand
Or speed beyond a mere man
To flee from your remand

I have no words that could say
Such measure as you can
And all the things I do bray
Are from a bragging man

My heart lies open to thee
To beat at your command
Or if you wish it to be
My heart of stone to sand

Such souls as there are sleeping
Are like this one of mine
The candle that I'm keeping
Its flame will hardly shine

I have no prayers that could
Fling open heaven's door
But only ask that you would
Help make my love grow more

I seek beyond no new day
Then that which I have now
For in thy hands I am clay
But a man if you allow

Chasing Jesus

Oh blessed holy town
Hear all your children crying
As Herod's swords are trying
To lay their young lives down

Oh blessed baby boy
Your saving grace is nearing
As Bethlehem is tearing
From parents loss of joy

Oh deathly hated night
When Herod's men came riding
To seek the one in hiding
Within the town of light

Oh children sought by death
Young martyrs to God's willing
That Herod's men were killing
To end the savior's breath

Oh baby Jesus cried
Which sent the angels flying
To souls of children dying
To lead them to God's side

Children of the Burning Bush

Come ye chosen David's men
Come into the devil's den
Cast thy sacred thoughts aside
Brace thyself for genocide

Lay thy children down to sleep
At the stairs to heavens keep
Thirsting lions wait to fill
From the flasks of whom they will

Come ye seedlings, taste the rain
In the fields of brother Cain
Hurl your cries upon the sky
From the ashes where you lie

Oh Exodus, thy holy quest
Took four tens in years to best
What price now for there to be
Oh Israel, oh home to thee

Come ye chosen David's men
Come into the devil's den
With thy millions hand in hand
Come and lie in Auschwitzland

Dawn

Perceive the light of dawn
That slowly spills into the night
Then strongly marches on

This chalice of God's love
Is poured before each coming day
By heaven's hand above

Oh blessed are my eyes
To witness this most sacred touch
Upon our earthly skies

I greet the newborn day
That proves forever holy truth
That God loves us each day

So grasp each morning's sight
For this is just a small, small part
Of God's eternal light

Earth's Twin

What vine has taken hold of me
What dust has filled my eye
Am I so rooted willingly
Beneath this earthly sky

I know I shouldn't value more
This clay of mortal breath
But God has made this world a lure
And men to suffer death

From mountain tops to oceans wide
With all that we could ever do
Will set a porous man astride
In wanting heaven, on earth too

But God's design and sacred plan
Is not about protecting earth
For it will pass and so must man
But in heaven, they'll both rebirth

So revere not this world we're in
And all the wonders God has sown
For there in heaven lies earth's twin
Safe beneath God's mighty throne

Faith

When evil comes before the eye
It'll burn the heart completely dry
Oh, what hails you from the pit
When temptation's fuse is lit

Wake the yards, the kids and wife
Wake the moon with song and fife
It's better to have a simple life
Than on the wings of strife

Guard your heart, guard your clay
Lest something takes your soul away
Oh, what whispers you would hear
If God should disappear

Shed all reasons you won't try
Shed the lumber in your eye
Faith is not a question why
Nor death as "Here I lie"

Hold to what you know is right
Hold to love to give it might
And when such evil comes at may
Trust your heart to turn away

Fallible

Cold as a winter's morning
Cold as the dead of night
Cold as the arctic's scorning
Is a heart that shuns all light

Deep as a baby's slumber
Deep as the wells of time
Deep as the stars in number
Are the souls who turned to crime

Let history show it's pages
On the decadence of man
For such had been for ages
Since atrocities began

From Eden's well known past
When Abel had been slain
Began a rift profoundly vast
When God cursed brother Cain

As far as an endless night
As far as the drifts of time
For never will a mortal light
See an end to the road we climb

Heaven's Call

Rejoice my friend, who's transcended the darkest night
And now can claim a better home, there in heaven's light

Go forth dear friend, and let your worries disappear
For time's sweet cloak ascends on you, there in heaven's sphere

Behold my friend, the angels sing to welcome you
As joyful songs distill the air, there in heaven's hue

Reach out dear friend, embrace of those from ages by
While memories sweeten the heart, there in heaven's sky

Exult my friend, no longer transience in wode-like flesh
Or succumbed to death's disquietude, there in heaven's crèche

Cry out dear friend, display the love we all agree
That endeared us all in loving you, there in heaven's lee

Elate my friend, for the heart of God shines thereof
With peace that fully soothes the soul, there in heaven's love

Reach out dear friend, take hold of Jesus' reaching hand
Who anoints you to his hallowed home, there in heaven's land

Rejoice my friend, and may your heart be ever blessed
As all your thirst be ever quenched, there at heaven's breast

He's Right There

Where is thy hand that steadies me
Where is thy voice that comforts me
Where, oh where, are you my lord
My God has gone away

Where is thy shield that shelters me
Where is thy sword that defends me
Where, oh where, are you my lord
My God has looked away

Where are thy tears in missing me
Where are thy fears in losing me
Where, oh where, are you my lord
My God has turned away

Where are thy arms to welcome me
Where is thy love to renew me
Where, oh where, are you my lord
My God has moved away

So who's been here in helping me
And who's been here in holding me
For here, right here, had been my lord
In the faces I see each day

Holy Ground

Let me walk on sacred ground
Upon the Mother's holy gown
Upon the green, upon the blue
Let me always cherish you

I can see the tailor's weaving
So alive and so believing
It is real, it is true
It is here for me and you

In the winter there's a potion
That will claim your stout devotion
Ever white, ever pearly
It will catch your breath quite surely

I can say beyond all guessing
That I've caught the good Lord's blessing
When I see, when I hold
Mother Nature's cherished gold

Let me feel the summer breeze
Beneath the sun's golden tease
Upon the sea, upon the earth
Let me value all it's worth

In my grasp, you've placed the handle
Of this treasured sacred candle
Burning bright, burning might
Keeping safe its precious light

Let me grow a little older
Walking by the good Lord's shoulder
Upon the green, upon the blue
Among the love that came from you

Jericho

Sing my men for victory
Sing my men for God
Sing that righteousness may see
Their flesh laid low to sod

Call for their surrendering
Call them to bow their heads
Call for God to swiftly bring
Their bones upon their beds

Hail the God of Israel
Hail the God of all
Hail the God who will unveil
Our way beyond the wall

Sing out your songs to be heard
Sing out your hearts with glee
Sing with the fury of his word
Then watch his sword run free

Oh hear our trumpets calling
Oh hear them loudly blow
Then hear the stones in falling
From the walls of Jericho

Judas

We did not know your role
That you were but the chosen one
And one with somber toll

For prophesy had said
That there shall be betrayal by
The one our Lord had fed

Thus Judas had been filled
With Satan's evil presence then
To have our Lord be killed

But now it's all so clear
That God had placed this onus on
Someone who he held dear

It had to be this way
For how else could our Lord fulfill
Salvation's passion play

Rejoice from dark and night
For Jesus knows the truth of it
And loves you still with might

Know Yourself

Oh how we battle between right and wrong
While obtusely engaged with the chaos of thought
So subtle sings the voice of the devil's song
That softly courts us to temptation's lot

We bear the demons that rest within
Who prey upon our wants and needs
Whose lies rest small on the scope of sin
But just big enough to plant their seeds

Slowly creeps the urges from dark into light
With a preponderance of stealth to veil its hunt
It seeks to appear as a natural insight
But with a slippery justice to its feral want

It's claimed to know better the demon we bare
While striving each day to subdue its need
Then to rid it completely from its fleshly lair
Allowing stronger ones to then intercede

Fear not the yearnings of the wicked we port
For our better angels have lent us their ear
It's far better to live with what we can thwart
Then to possibly acquire something more severe

Luke 11:24-25

Peter

What lies my mouth had told
That billowed out upon their own
Like thieves seduced by gold

How could I've given in
By fears to save my mortal life
Denying all again

For thrice my words rang out
And thrice my shame had smitten me
Before the rooster's shout

Oh what a fool am I
To think I wouldn't turn from him
When danger was most high

This thirst for corporeal breath
That even Jesus knew I held
Spurred me in fearing death

He knew what would take place
He knew the depths of time itself
Yet still, he gave me grace

Purgatory Road

This road has no night or day
It goes where heaven tells it
And has no other turn or say
To those who walk upon it

Step by weary step they go
While giving voice to prayer
Piety is all they show
Their past so bluntly bare

Behold their endless questing
To achieve this solemn chore
Whose fare is never resting
But to ceaselessly endure

It's all about reflection
And a need to bring a soul
To spiritual perfection
Transformation is its goal

So take heed my mortal friend
Less you find yourself to bode
On that solitary end
That is purgatory road

The Birth

I stand upon hallowed ground
With all my senses turned around
His holy cry had softened me
To walk the path of honesty

Wrong is wrong, and right is right
And always light surpasses night
I shake with joy as angels sing
For here I stand before the king

And with his little hand in mine
His smiling face was pure sunshine
I felt the love within his sight
That flowed impartial with such might

While through the night the stars stood by
By shouting out their names from high
This honor they'd bestowed on you
Was all because God's word came true

I quivered at a shepherd's horn
Proclaiming that the king was born
So safe was Jesus in their keep
As angels sang him off to sleep

Thus on this night my past was shorn
For I had seen our savior born

The Centurion

Upon my soul I swear it's true that what transpired
thereon that day was not absurd
But rather it was preordained by scriptures that had
strengthen this through holy word

My day was like all other days, so filled with thoughts
of duty and of servitude
That I knew not that destiny awaited me in ever grow-
ing magnitude

For even as I write these words, I tremble with the
shameful thoughts of what I've done
While knowing that forever now all living men will call
me as the cursed one

Although I did what I have done for many years with-
out a qualm or second thought
That morning when I paused to look within his pierc-
ing eyes, I gravely felt distraught

For never had I felt compelled to speak aloud on my
behalf, in what I do
Yet when I placed upon his back that bane of wood, my
voice had failed to follow through

Therefore I followed in his wake, determined to
address this man eventually
While hearing all the taunts and jeers that he endured
upon his road to Calgary

Perhaps if I had fled right there, then I would be far
better off than I am now
But I was bound by duty and to duty I'm beholden to
completely bow

Thus when we laid him on that cross that he had bore
with hardship up that long, steep hill
I still had not the question that I felt inside, nor did I
find my voice with will

My barren eyes beheld a sting that came from more
than just the sweat upon my brow
Which seemed to march in tandem with the subtle
quakes my body now exudes somehow

Thus when I placed the nail against his sticky flesh to
callously await the blow
I felt myself bestirring from this ghoulish sleep, that
time had ever held me so

For ne'er before had I perceived the impact that my
morbid work had played on me
Because I kept aloft of all the pain I caused and
brought about so casually

What godly spell did this man used to make me see
beyond the world I thought I knew
For he not once had said a word, and yet his eyes
benignly watched what I would do

Then as I brought the hammer down to drive the
spike far into him, it felt instead
That I had drove it into me, and flooded all my
being with a scourging dread

Somehow I pressed myself to last and bring this
horrid chore to end, that I've begun
But with each savage hammer blow, another piece
of my poor soul had come undone

And when another placed thereon his sagging head a
crown of thorns, and called him king
I barely had the strength to stand while there above
our judging eyes, the cross took wing

His pain was such that even those who shared the sky
on crosses of their very own
Proclaimed that it was quite unjust for such as he
whose guilt was less, to be condoned

I marveled at their chosen words, and saw the truth of
what they said to this bound man
Who hadn't spoken any word, but now he offered more
than what a person can

What had this man believing that he was who he had
claimed to be, so ardently
And then to shake my very earth, when they
proclaimed him savior all so eagerly

Then to the heavens he reached out, with words that
made me want to weep on bended knee
Have mercy father on them all, for they know not of
what they do to you and me

If I could shrink, then I would be the smallest creature
that the land had ever had
For I was so ashamed of this, my part in what took
place today, was simply mad

But there was more to my demise, for with his last and
final breath, I was to tend
By plunging forth my trusted spear into his lungs to
verify, this had an end

And as my trembling hands retreat, the skies grew
dark with thunder raging on our ears
Which rose in tandem to the earth's great quaking
that I've never seen in all my years

Oh this was surely God's true son, which now my
voice had finally, been loosened free
And I, the one who heinously had brought about his
ending so abhorrently

I am a man whose grim held role, will bring no light to
this dark world that we live in
Soldier of a vile profession, who offers death to all the
love we keep within

Why couldn't I step back that day from such a fated ill
lead deed, I've often ask
But only found my answer in, that I was not enlight-
ened till I did my task

Sometimes the weight of what I've done suppresses all
my thirst for life, to seek an end
By falling on the very spear that I had used to finish
him, my only friend

His knowing eyes had not the least of any kind of hate
or scorn to lay on me
But rather there was only love and sorrow that he
showered me in sympathy

Why has my world been turned about and why did it
abide, until my trial with him
Had God decided to seek out my actual life, or was it
just a godly whim

Where is the heaven I need too, that now evades my
chastened heart and tainted soul
Is there no cross that I could bare, that then could
take me from this hell that I now troll

For even now I feel the looks that others pose upon
this wretched world I walk
And hear the whispers of their scorn and all the curses
they would utter or would hawk

Oh how my life is tossed about as if the winds of all the
earth had hold of me
To ever roam a salted path of bleeding blood that
grants this curse finality

For never will I see again the world that I had once
knew well, and carelessly
Since I've been touched by no one's hand, but still
been felled by something more extensively

The Comforting of Saul

What chastely sound is this
That fills the air with tenderness
And brings my spirit bliss

Such music I must swill
With all the hardiness of will
My seeking has no fill

No other sagely spell
Could calm the fury sent by hell
As does this boy so well

With chosen instrument
Which long has been so pertinent
For angels choiring vent

Within my troubled reign
A demon harkens me to strain
Against the part that's sane

But when my ears behold
His songs that ooze of heaven's gold
My heart becomes less cold

I must have in my keep
This boy who plays for men and sheep
Who eased my nights to sleep

Come forth dear lad and know
That I, King Saul, shall make it so
This honor I bestow

The Failing

Forever and a day go I
With longing in my heart
Ever pursued by the question why
From God must I so part

Each lonely step I take
Each day by graceless day
I languor on this road I make
Resigned to stay away

How much is heaven weeping
To watch my soul in stress
For sins my shame is keeping
Me from seeking to confess

Where does the veil get parted
When will my voice be set
How can I get this started
If I feel it's not time yet

Each day into tomorrow
Less time to make a stand
More deeper runs my sorrow
And much nearer God at hand

The Stigma of Sin

I will heed no thoughts of worthless spinning
To the words I've forged to show I'm winning
For I'll bare my heart for endless skinning
On the altar of my love

Never will my faith have restitution
Or desiring vengeful revolution
When my soul is crying for some solution
From the Lord who reigns above

Carry not my bag of faults I weathered
Filled with countless sins that I had gathered
For the mirrored face is where it's levered
On the cross that I must bare

Let the rain pour down on my perdition
Wash away my tears of long attrition
From the guilt my spirit must audition
Of the sins that keep me there

Thrice

I know not of this man
Nor of those men he brought along
Mistake me not, his clan

But hold, a voice cried more
For surely you're from Galilee
I've seen you both before

Take leave your hands on me
For I know not this chosen one
Now go and let me be

Yet still the crowd gave chase
To thrice accuse of him to know
The man at Herod's place

Again I will deny
I have no dealings with this man
Appeased, the crowd slipped by

But one would not abide
Who crowed the coming of the dawn
At which, poor Peter cried

Through the Valley

Through the dark most waspy marrow
That cloaks a soul in gasping carol
Sings the song from those departed
Through the valley all disheartened

Away, away, a way is offered
Yet all your guilt is justly coffered
Holding thee to ponder breath
There within the valley death

So take thy shame when memory purges
And wear the mantel sin now urges
For this must pass if there'll be passing
From the dark of spirits massing

Yet hope still wallows in this night
For eyes still seeking for the light
While time will ferry you away
The Lord still wait to hear you pray

But when all needs are finally one
When juxtaposition has begun
Then see the light, the love, the way
And pass through heaven's gate at may

Upon the Hill

I hear oh Lord, a voice so distant crying
I feel oh Lord, a wind so warmly sighing
So I looked there, upon the hill
Where time's been stricken still

I hear oh Lord, the earth beneath me sighing
I feel oh Lord, the fields that now are dying
But I looked there, upon the hill
And knew the sun, shone still

I see oh Lord, a darkly cloud is coming
I hear oh Lord, a drummer's steady drumming
But looking there, upon the hill
I felt my heart take will

I see oh Lord, a sword that's slowing rising
I hear oh Lord, that nations are surmising
But looking there, upon the hill
I trust your reigning will

I fear oh Lord, an awesome toll is coming
I hear oh Lord, a change within the drumming
But waiting there, upon the hill
Your heart does bleed, yet still

I fear oh Lord, my death at each horizon
I fear oh Lord, my soul abruptly rising
But waiting there, upon the hill
Your love is with me still

Hate, Evil and Anger...

A Mind in Doubt

Murder has a way of sneaking up
And branding you in its fire
Like a lazy river waking up
Flooding you with desire

Nothing will ever, just fade away
Like a morning's early frost
It'll wait for a match to light its way
And to hell with what it will cost

Then once the devil's been turned out
The curtain's drawn again
For the conscience of a mind in doubt
Must justify his sin

Killing, has no morality
It's a straw that's grasped by few
But feasts on anger's reality
And its raging point of view

Reactions can be temperamental
When triggered by true surprise
With results that spurn the sentimental
Leaving death to cloud the eyes

An Offal Cuisine

Will I be back tomorrow since the sorrows I had given
To add in flavor to the pot I've boiled
With a pinching of true madness in the stew that I have fashioned
Of a bitterroot that doesn't feel regret

Will I bring a fork for stirring in the salt that I would offer
And ladle it upon the wounds I've made
Then have you look into my eyes to see my cooking pleasure
The apple that will gloat within your eye

Will you become annoyed to find, my serving has been tempered
By feeding you a spoonful at a time
I'm hoping that the taste you tongued has found its proper seasoning
By bringing back a cud-like tenderness

So wallow in this fashioned meal, of misery and displeasure
For I am not your angel in disguise
I'll dish out all my seething rage, with ever needed vengeance
And hope your life's forever in my stew

Angry Need

What mark has yonder dagger set
Where it shall pierce my living flesh
For in your hate your eyes have yet
Seen truth where lies are still so fresh

This falsehood cloak you hide within
Has turned your heart forever bare
And caused your ears to not give in
To words that could then make you care

Are you so blind that you can't see
Beyond the pain that smothers you
For life will never quite agree
If you insist in what you're due

We've spoken much, but little said
With words that say not near enough
For all the sorrys I have bled
Yet still you seek my heart to cuff

Take hold my friend onto your cross
And bare it well on this sore deed
For I do know it was your loss
That led you to this angry need

Evil Uses, Abuses and Kills

The world has seen the rising of a new and deadly threat
Of a terroristic evil using lies within its net

It had taken hold of many through religious sentiment
And had falsely used these standards for Jihadist temperament

They have shed the blood of innocents and fed upon their fear
While they scorned the badge of justice since their hate is all they
cheer

Yet the people who they prey upon, can say they're not alone
For they've twisted those enlisted on the lies that they had sown

In their rush to claim religion as the cause for their crusade
They have mocked Islamic virtues through the use of this charade

So take hold of one another and pursue this to all ends
For we must destroy this evil and the terror it extends

Hold Back the Dark

Where are the boundaries tween good and evil
Where are the ones who would turn you around
When our spirits had fallen from all understanding
Who'd focus the light, for us to be found

The ages will wane of detestable miscues
Witness to those who mishandle their lives
Choices that were self righteously taken
Thus warming the bed where evil now thrives

Where are the bars for holding back anger
Where are the limits that rage won't pursue
When justice had lost its way to see clearly
Who would then guide our eyes to what's true

Time is the theatre of Satan's endeavors
Enveloped forever by all of his lies
Destined to have it ever repeating
Such is the course our history applies

Where are the words that need to be spoken
Where is the wisdom that needs to be found
Only when hearts of goodness awaken
Will hold back the dark of evil unbound

Incessant

As if the dark of night
Could cloak his acts and ease the pain
While in perverse delight

Such is his stricken yen
To use the night to hide his guilt
And then, each night again

Within his mind he knows
That what he does is very wrong
Yet still his hunger grows

His ears had long ignored
The sobbing sounds that whimpered from
The child that he adored

While there upon his lips
The lies he's told to soothe himself
Will lash his child as whips

What anchor holds him fast
That point of view which keeps him sane
Beyond his raging past

How blind that he can't see
Those eyes which plead beneath his lust
Cry forth to be set free

Oh lonely, cornered child
Let not your father's path guide you
To stray forever wild

Psychosis

I look out at all of those faces
There're none who have any love for me
All that I see, is all of my pain
That feeds my desire to run away

But there is no solace for me on the road
The feigning faces are everywhere
They stare as if I were the hound
With their smothering and hovering, judging looks

They know not I, as I know myself
Yet they taunt me with their empty eyes
A swarth of darkness consumes my heart
While all my thoughts are woven in ashes

My madness lives within my cup
With a never ending thirst, going unfulfilled
Boldly my hands take hold of the answer
A sharp steely edge of blade to whet

Oh, how they press in so closely on me
This pressure that I, now must realign
If I can't part from these damning faces
Then they damn well must part from me

Simmering Innocence

The court has spoken clearly
My verdict stuns and shreds my faith
And wronged me so severely

For justice marched in blindly
Into the field to meddle out
A measure so unkindly

I lapse into a funnel
That pulls upon my sanity
As dark as any tunnel

And in such dismal thinking
I felt the first of many tugs
That led all hope to sinking

But time has made me stronger
Eight years have passed since I've been judged
My stay will not be longer

These years have ripped asunder
My life into a vengeful quest
Embracing distant thunder

No end has blessed my grieving
Forever I'll stand nakedly
As then at my deceiving

My temper heeds no calling
Nor any patience's cooling breeze
Or reason's subtle stalling

This eye will cost another
While in my mouth a sourness
My teeth demand their brother

Exodus 21:24

The Chimney Tree

I stand before the raven
I stand before the chimney tree
For all my years at slaving
Tis freedom be the death of me

Burn, voiced the raven's scree
Burn, voiced the dark of night
Only ghosts tonight are free
Riding in their sheets of white

Near to thee I'm risen up
Above this devils' thunder
Soon the raven's call to sup
Will start the pyre like plunder

I hang before their hating eyes
I hang upon that tree
A noose holds back my pleading cries
As fire takes hold of me

Burn, said the men in white
And burning's what they gave
Hate rules the devil's night
As weeping angels rave

What Dark Unleashes

It hides as though asleep
And lies within the shadows of the corner of your mind

Unheard, unseen, and deep
And all aware of every thought, like a hunter in a blind

No righteous mind goes there
There within the hidden pool, where evil likes to rest

It sits and waits to flair
Waiting for the heart to break, when shattered nerves will crest

That's when what dark unleashes
To put to torch all common sense as self control unwound

Then sally forth these leeches
Cutting words that hurt so deep, or deeds so cruelly bound

Shorts...

A Silent Reflection

To silence working, a silent pay
For those who thrive to live that way

And they who seek that solemn shield
Silence, will be their lasting yield

To silence seed, a silent weed
Cause nothing grows in silent need

For emptiness is what it reels
The only thing that silence feels

Another Day

I envy thee thy restful sleep
No more shall there be tears to weep
And of your love that ran so deep
It shines in heaven's keep

Within my heart I'll bare this woe
Because my friend I'd came to know
That smile of yours you'd often show
In friendship long ago

So blessed be thy going way
While always in my mind will stay
Those words that we would often say
We'll meet another day

Carrion's Creed

To the damned comes the deed
Riding in on hell bent steed

Let all the wary watch its passing
And try to stay their tongue from asking

Of fortunes gained and fortunes lost
It's to the damned their souls will cost

To cry their hearts forever and ever
And of God's blessing, never

In Wet Seasons

Let not our tears go to waste
That we had shed face to face

It's only natural for us to stumble
Even islands and rocks can crumble

Of all the tears that ease our pain
To cry, can give us much to gain

So let your tears fall on my shoulder
And life will be, that much less colder

Infinite Affinity

Like the magic of a rainbow
Or the crowning of a king
Whenever you are near me
It can match no other thing

Like the strength of a mighty river
Or the warmth of a summer sun
I grow in the love you've shown me
The miracle you've begun

My Lady Love

My lady love, my lady of, enticing dimensions
My lady dove, so full of love, she eases my tensions

She carries my heart, my love, my flame
There's no other aim than her love to claim

A morning sky, a rooster's cry, a new day is here
Another try for you and I, a new life so dear

She'll know it is true, my love how it grew
And so will she too, loving me, loving you

No Blindfold Please

How can you doubt, and then, in doubt to end
Is revenge so sweet, so badly needed, to me your friend

Oh how I wail to the pain of it all
Helpless within the box, to Pandora's call

I lack the fuel to light my will
Yet still I take it all, yet still

My love's intact, unchanged, unmoved
It always will be, and with only that, I'm soothed

Rio

Well I wish I had tomorrow, to worry with today
Cause today I just don't have enough for it to simply pay

So I hope to see some trouble, come dropping in my way
Cause this mood that I've developed, just seems to want to stay

Since my girl has gone to Rio, nothing matters anymore
I can't find enough of trouble, or a heart without a whore

The Inevitable

The inevitable will soon be the past
The ascension to a man, through the follies of youth
Will soon come about at last

Why hurry the surety of years
Has time rolled forth even part of its ilk
Rush not young child with your fears

With purpose our youth is given
For soon the trappings of adulthood worries
Will dominate all of your livin

The Wage of Vengeance

Upon thy pain, your heart will bleed
But on your talons rest your need

No stone shall lie without your touch
Until thy sweet revenge is such

But only short will last your ease
For in thy chosen cloak will breeze

A wind to sing a song so old
That leaves the soul forever cold

What We Are

Will the stars come out tonight and shine within her eyes
To sparkle so enchantingly, they sure can hypnotize

And will her touch send tremors racing up and down my spine
As convulsively I'll quiver as if drunk on potent wine

While lying in your arms I feel the strength of what we are
Two lovers destined from the start, and destined to go far

Miscellaneous...

Anxiety

Sleep, that haven that we all flee to
How can I now consider sleep
Is not the world so perched askew
To threaten all I do

Sleep, that comfort which now runs away
As if its caging doors thrown wide
What part of me would I betray
To thus find sleep at may

Nay, do I say to that slumbering god
Who calls us all into his keep
No longer shall my worldly trod
March evenly abroad

This peril I shall now adopt
From woes that ever press on me
Around and around my world will flop
And I, the spinning top

Sleep, while all my luck has run so dry
No way will I be giving in
Not while my troubles cry and cry
Less from this world I fly

Oh sleep, oh how I wish so deep
Perhaps, I will succumb to thee
But to that endless night so steep
To rest forever in thy keep

Feud

He walked through the doorway and into the room
With footsteps so soft yet boding of doom
He neither looked left nor off to his right
But straight to my table with me in his sight

His mouth held a grimness that told me instead
He expected tomorrow would find him quite dead
Yet I knew from the stare he gave me this night
There would be no running or ducking this fight

Brother, dear brother, I won't question why
You seek out another, an eye for an eye
Brother, dear brother, you know that it's true
Wherever you go, is where I go too

His eyes held a fire that shimmered in red
Which spoke of the hell his fury was fed
What drove him this much to bring him my way
To stand here before me with no words to say

Then nodding my head with one lasting sigh
I rose to my feet still meeting his eye
And when he did walk through that doorway again
We went side by side, to lose or to win

Brother, dear brother, I won't question why
You seek out another, an eye for an eye
Brother, dear brother, you know that it's true
Whoever you're fighting, then I'm fighting too

Comes the End

Like wool that shrouds a poor fool's sight
My eyes betray me
All my horrors still are livin
All my sorrows keep me driven
Panic engulfs me

Loudly rings the note of irony
Gripping at my heart
As the bell tolls the grave's fixed hour
I cringe in fear of its grim power
Telling me to part

A crescendo of bees nestle near
Taking all my breath
Upheavals rock my earthly chest
As giants settle on my breast
Reaching forth is death

Cold, cold fingers enclose around me
Clasped as winter's friend
Swiftly the past races by
All in the blinking of an eye
And then comes, the end

It's a Tough Job, But Someone Has To Do It

The tethers on my reindeer
Are wearing pretty thin
It seems like only last year
That I had them fixed again

With every coming Christmas
Repairs are needed more
And of my fix it up list
It's harder to endure

The runners on my sleigh are
Crooked and quite bent
Much like a family's old car
Its undercoating's spent

It needs another paint job
But I haven't found the time
The bells upon the doorknob
They clang instead of rhyme

And then there's poor ole Rudolph
Whose nose had always shined
He suffers from a bad cough
And starting to go blind

My elves are all so weary
From all the work they do
Their faces lack those cheery
Bright smiles I once had too

More kids each year are writing
And I simply can't refuse
It only keeps igniting
My wretched Christmas blues

My age is three oh seven
My looks are fifty two
But I feel like eight eleven
From this job that I pursue

But who could bring each season
A Christmas without flaws
This joy gives me the reason
For being Santa Claus

Man in the Moon

Come one, come all, but all beware
Of a lonely old man with a timeless stare
Who'll watch as the follies of women and men
Be ever repeated again and again

Pale is the light that lights his face
Grim is the home he calls his place
And every night he'll follow you
From east to west, he will pursue

Bright are the stars that crown him king
Loud are the wolves to whom they sing
But do beware what he'll unfold
A magic so old, so timeless and gold

So look to the sky for the traveling loon
Forever he's known as the man in the moon

My Mistress

Our hearts were weary, with bodies tired
The waves kept coming, and seas were mired
With weather's wintry and tempest breath
Twill only bring us close to death

Yet still we ride the raging seas
Longing to get home to you

Through tossing waves and thunderous nights
The ship would pitch to her delights
Our mistress held us in her cup
And if she deign, could swallow us up

Yet still we held to spar and trim
Longing to sail home to you

At night the ghosts would walk about
They were the dead that she called out
Good faithful men to her and crew
Good sailors who she dressed in blue

Yet still we sailed through salty dew
Longing to hold onto you

For months we tacked upon her skirt
Our mistress who could love or hurt
It made our love so bittersweet
For once we're home, we're incomplete

Yet still we knew we would again
Be leaving once more for you

So farewell good woman, farewell my wife
I leave again for my sailing life
I'll miss you deeply, I'll miss you true
But I miss my mistress ocean blue

Yet still I yearn for both my loves
Longing for each of you

Service Before Self

Where most mortals often fear to tread
God's angels dare to step right in
When men must face unbearable dread
There are very few who'd answer then

Life has its moments of ups and downs
With dangers that you can't run from
But only those vested in saintly crowns
March to the beat of another drum

When valor's call is soundly tendered
Who would answer its needful cry
For the price of service may be rendered
At far greater cost to those who try

Within us all, a spirit's residing
That can, or can not, move us to act
For most, when threats urge braver striding
Only the selfless will rise to the fact

Behold the touch of God's stretched hand
Bringing his blessing to the chosen few
They are the ones who heed the demand
To risk it all, and their lives for you

Sparing the King's Rod

What's that I say, in lean array
Of childish words that spat and spray
What's that I mean, I'll make a scene
Just selfish wants with no between

I'll prance before thy grudging eye
No reason why I fake my cry
Just child-like wails to sting thy ears
With senseless tears to rout my peers

What's that I need, with all due speed
A kingly whipping to proceed
What's that I get, a listless hit
Which thus begun a royal fit

But ne'er again did come to be
A time to flee, the rod for me
And ne'er again I had to wince
For I was since, a spoiled prince

Stew

Into the briar patch you go
Safe from every danger
Quick are your feet that take you there
Far from any stranger
Hoarse are the hounds seeking you
Blind are their eyes to see
Deep in the briar patch you wait
For night to set you free

Resting little rabbit
Testing those out there
Silence is your habit
Violence you must fare

Into the briar patch they try
To push their way to you
Finding the thorns too much to bear
Then eager on leaving too
Soon come the hunters hunting you
To quiet down the hounds
Then forcing their way to where you lie
They catch you in its bounds

Hasty little rabbit
Tasty in a stew
Taken to the abbot
And cooked through and through

The Eve of November

Oh, night
Oh, darkness of dreaded eve
What poised plan do thy witches brew
With skulking chants their craft will hew
And who will on this eve lay check
Gainst unseen swells that chill the neck

Call, ravens
Congeal the night
As all your brethren sit in fright
Except the owl, who watches all
And to the wayfarer, his call

Oh, wind
How became your slurring way
What force has drawn you thin and slow
To wail through forests as you go
Yet in the moonlit empty sky
Unleashed, you'll let the clouds race by

Rise, Pluto
And hail your tendered lot
Who on this night have fled the plot
With wispy tendrils craving all
The ghosts of many come to call

Beware, children
The gulf of this one night
For it will reach out to receive
Young fledglings whom it will deceive
Abhor the feigning cries the most
Disguised as what your parents host

Oh, quicken sleep
Awaken from thy slumber
Let us refrain our sheep to number
For vigilance we must remember
On every eve of November

The Highwayman

I am a rogue of dubious intentions
With fealty to my own heart
Although my role has hubris pretentions
It's to my needs, I play this part

Where I would go are grievous petitions
For the parting of someone's gold
Yet all my joy from previous additions
Were better spent in tales I told

I am a rogue of marvelous perception
Whose only care is in your purse
My greatest trait is obvious deception
I'll leave you dry or even worse

Take care to shun my fallacious appearance
Less you become my ball of yarn
I rule the road with malicious adherence
And would hang your corpse in any barn

The Legend Waits

Buried beneath the ground, beneath the ashes, from distant sound
He lies there in the deep, timelessly asleep, within his keep

Leathery hide for haunches
Leathery hide for feet
Leathery hide that hid it all
A cask of fire and heat

His caverns deeply reminisce, the horrid screams, the smoky hiss
As young fair maidens in their gowns, were brought from nearby
towns

Gathered in veils of white
Gathered in blossoms too
Gathered in deathly fright
Then gathered in jaws that chew

Within the bowels of fissured earth, within his lair, his sleeping berth
Time bestirs his waking breath, of sleeping steel, and rousing death

As legend will hide the horror
And legend will hide the fears
But legend will come tomorrow
When the dragon soon appears

The Night I Sang Dixie

I ran like an Alpha in a buffed out wolfpack
No scrimping the pimping to the clothes on my back
I rolled in my Caddy like a Hollywood star
With my posse of homies riding there in my car

So smooth was the action, when my game face was on
I was the prince of all players and a boo's Don Juan

Then one night I was hooked on a strawberry blonde
Catching flies with my honey in her dippy-do pond
When a light so brightly shot straight from the sky
Falling fast on my ass, like a blitzing banzai

My mouth hurled a "What?" like a vending machine
While parked in a forest, I was making a scene

Then slicker than a kid on a greased potty chair
My ass was arising, hauling me through the air
Meanwhile I heard screeching, engulfing the night
But my boo was just gaping, at my hysterics in flight

So I quickly shut down my girlyman scream
And regained some cool in the midst of that beam

Then before I knew it, I was caught in their ship
Where three anxious aliens, had a probe in their grip
And that was the night I was tossed in the can
Singing out like a lark, just a Dixie Tarzan

The Reaper and the Reaped

I've read your thoughts, your prose my friend
And found myself at your wit's end

Such agony in words you cry
Has shown your heart's despairing sigh

Your anguished soul has been writ down
To smote all passing readers found

As if the tempest of your grief
Could reach right out and stir belief

Yet as I read and wrest with thee
I find myself, no longer me

I find myself with heart in throat
With all your hurts as mine to tote

The Reel of Time

Each day that passes, another one rises
And never the future be nearer
For each day gained, has no disguises
Yet still the future's no clearer

These temporal bonds that hold us here
That wedge us between what was and what will
It's why all of life must so adhere
To each moment upon time's reel

Yet all our senses struggle to know
What speed, what distance, does time apply
Are we all moving immensely slow
Or faster than a blink of an eye

Time was, time is, time always will be
Immeasurable and unending
Vast are the realms of tomorrow's scree
But today, only one's transcending

Each moment passes, another one arrives
And we must experience them all
For each moment gained, brings all our lives
Past memories to view in recall

The Skrimschawer

When twilight dims before the dawn of night
And the sky gives ground to the stars most bright
That's when you heed the old, old warning
Take shelter until next morning

For that's the time when the wind grows still
When the silence tarries in the woods at will
And you know deep down that time's withdrawing
Take shelter before the culling

And when all the doors have been closed and blocked
When the window shutters have been safely locked
That's when your heart is swiftly drumming
Take shelter, for it is coming

Long are the legs that carry it
Long are the arms by its side
Sharp are the teeth that barely fit
In a jaw that is two feet wide

Foul is the stench it carries
Foul is the yield of its breath
Dark is the blood it ferries
In a husk that craves on death

When the shadows dance to the pale moon's light
And your heart's ensnared by the fear you fight
That's when you need to race like a deer
Take shelter, for it is near

When the hair on your arms turns suddenly cold
From a breaking branch that the woods unfold
That's when you know that it's far too late
For shelter has locked its gate

The Traveling Man

Who can watch the play of stars
Or the snaking tide of living cars
Who can taste from nature's breast
Across the land at every crest
Or feel the soothing, golden sun
Shortly aft each day's begun

It's the traveling man
Tis he who can
He counts his blessings
To be where he can

And who can see the hill turn valley
Or in the city, the street to alley
Who can hear the desert's singing
From rain that any storm was bringing
Or trekked a beach to where it goes
With flowing sand between the toes

It's the traveling man
Tis he who can
He count his blessings
To be where he can

It's he who've seen the tree turn forest
Or heard the crickets' noble chorus
And followed mountain spring to river
Through summer's heat or winter's shiver
It's he who walked such countless trails
And blessed to tell a thousand tales

For if I could be such a man
I'd count my blessings
To be where I can

Time's First Step

Seconds, are just a short bit of time
They're here, and then so quickly gone
Hardly do we notice their subtle climb
They come, they go, and on and on

Can time be ever flawlessly measured
With a second divided, again and again
For where does lie the final bit treasured
Where time's first step could first begin

No made device could ever catch it
Or photograph its watershed
Only God has the means to firmly hold it
Because he is the actual roadbed

If time could be pared to its smallest part
What name, what term, would we then use
This temporal rift where time would start
Has held the secret to paths we choose

Wheaton's Way

Wheaton's way was always gray
Steeped in dour moods that bray
Much a man whose night is day
Much a man of Loki's clay

Wheaton's words were quite absurd
Among the ears of those who've heard
But in the rafters they had spurred
A grackle's caw that they bestirred

Wheaton's will was always ill
Upon the waters ever still
But never on the daffodil
That gathered wild upon his hill

Wheaton's ghost was always host
Unto the annuls time would boast
And read to all as his impost
I shun the hearts that bleed the most

Wheaton's heart was always dark
He lived a life forever stark
For love had never made a mark
And death, his only joyful spark

With Sand in My Hand

I'll come within your night
To work my magic wonder
My touch is sure and right
And in subconscious light
I'll put you deeply under

May all your prayers be said
Lest in this night you wander
And find yourself in dread
In worlds that fill your head
Of visions full of thunder

Yet woes are not my song
I sing the theme of plunder
Of hidden needs you long
No matter right or wrong
Your consciousness is under

So drink this cup I measure
Let not your sleep be late
But grasp this mystic treasure
Be it dread, or be it pleasure
You can not make it wait

Now herald forth the sheep
For nights were meant for sleeping
And offer me my keep
My fee for blessed sleep
Are dreams that you are reaping

An Abbreviated Memoir of Trial and Tribulation...

South of Heaven, North of Hell

The truth is never welcomed in a stoic heart, but unto this
truth, most of all
For it had taken me a lifetime to learn this, and to finally
heed its call

Each spoken word, each lauded sound, all living noise that's
been set forth, is never gone
But is captured upon the wind and carried through the
drifts of time, forever on

Henceforth my words from all my days had ne'er been lost,
but rest upon the gifted air
To ride thereon those tides of time, locked away while ever
waiting the Lord to share

This is, and was, how life must go, as God looked on our
blunted souls, and worldly pew
Destined to be always watched, and marked into the book of
life our lord would view

Whereby began my journey here, for borne into lavation's
light, I came to be
Then placed within the mold of flesh, and fated to those
mortal tracks, to race carefree

I entered the world of man, flawed in every way, yet knowing
not of guilt at all
For innocence had clothed my soul, yet still I wore the mark
of sin from Eden's fall

So hear my tale, live my story, for it is one of countless falls
into the dark
For I have walked a hidden path of twistedness, where sin
and earthly wanting hark

Thus marched the threads of zoetic time, that grew so
symbiotic to my mortal need
Not yet the man who I will be, I ran with childish aimless-
ness in reckless speed

So young with youth and bold with game, my foolishness
ruled thoroughly my thinking heart
It was an age of puzzles and discoveries, with answers
shown in partial part

All learning came amended of its levied cost, as wisdom's
blade performed its cut
Sublime in power, complete in venue, and quite oblivious to
where we strut

For living was the means to the things we wanted, and dared
us to reach to extremes
Bigger, better, and selfishly bent, it had led us to chase our
most daring of dreams

But then came the days when I found my misgivings, and
heard what my heart had to say
And entered the world where my parents true teachings,
unfolded God's script to my play

This road that rushed below my feet, that slacked my thirst
in ways that quenched my shattered soul
Had just as quickly filled my heart with such degree, a fugue
of loathing as my toll

It could be said by some who see it differently, should it be
known of what I've done
That I was young and immature, and would disparage all
behavior, homeward spun

But this is not a bourgeois tale, nor of family failing in its
duties here
For I was raised in righteous love, by parents who did all
they could each growing year

Hence I could say it's more than fair, that others would
assuredly turn their eyes away
By stepping back in total shock, to cross their hearts at
what could darken me this way

Thus raced the years of faults and flaws, while I delayed all
efforts to attain amends
For procrastination's comfort had snuggled me, giving way
to my wanton trends

Then came that time where I achieved transitioning unto the
fellowship of man
And though I'd passed this corporal rite of being grown, my
adulthood still lacked its span

Yet even though I now could claim the right to do
whatever I desired for me
I still was not mature enough, to understand the conse-
quences in degree

Yet changes did come grudgingly eventually, as stubborn as
my nature knew
And though my heart knew what was right, it was a lack in
spirit leaving me askew

So unperceiving I've become, from a focus so corrupted by
vanity
That barely could I recognize my given face, in the mirror
that mirrored me

Thus as I wallowed through life's mire, two changes of signif-
icance had came about
And found myself not only wed, but blessed in claiming a
new faith, had called me out

For I was sure that from this church I'd now embraced,
would be and was what I desired
And gave to me that needed draught, that I so much had
ever longed to be inspired

It was for me a blessed time, to which I now could see myself
grow righteously
And took my first big forward step in baptism, where it
before avoided me

My joy at this turned all my life's tart vinegar into a bliss, for
I'm transposed
As vivid sins were washed away in baptismal waters,
forever now disposed

But all my gains would soon be doomed, for differences had
strongly bent our lives around
And set our course tumultuously upon a road, that slowly
beat our feelings down

For marriage thrived in bitter heat, and left us both to
languor on the crust of love
That often spiraled uncontained, and led me less from righ-
teousness that I know of

Then came a time unrivaled by any blessing, and the father
in me was born
And forever there after my heart was awoken, to the children
I love and adorn

Whereby my years had finally found life's golden crown, as
maturity settled in
Yet with that crown I grew aware how gravely been my list-
lessness to all my sin

It left me hulled by guilt and fear that washed away my will-
ingness to make things right
And set me slowly poised to drown, unable to forgive myself
in heaven's sight

But I did learn to persevere against my muddled nature as
the years marched by
Yet still I failed to look into God's watching eye, while know-
ing he was asking why

No longer did I savor church, for I had drifted from its
bounds in servitude
And once again had lost myself, to swallow hard upon the
discord I've accrued

I watched as life's chaotic essence swirl about, as it would
torque what mattered most
As friction reared from what it wrought, it would be of my
family that paid foremost

Such were the times when darkness reigned and joy grew
faint, as love was just a shadow of
While thoughts were where they shouldn't lie, far from the
realms where angels cry and mourn above

My world was etched by love and hate, for I was now unable
to step back at all
And teetered there upon the brink, and knew that it would
take God's hand to stop my fall

And fall I did, but not in all, for life's penchant for dissolution was diffuse
By offering an alternate reality, and new beginning to unloose

Sometimes our love can fade away when differences have grown beyond our will to stay
Thus poisoning the very ground on which we stand, and causing us to die that way

Although it sadden me in part, it was the hand I truly yearned for saving me
And thus began my new found life, with love far deeper than I thought I'd ever see

For I now took a road away, from all the angry viciousness that we displayed
And left behind the welts and scars, that bitterness and emptiness had fully laid

Yet I was blessed to see a ray of Cupid's light that over time grew mightily
And found that love once more took back, control of all those weaknesses I had in me

With marriage lost, but love regained, I now won back that part of me that I let go
And finally could be myself, allowing all the good in me to rise and glow

Yet even though these changes were significant, there still were subtle fallacies
For I still had my vanity, as well as all my selfishness in broad degrees

Although I struggled to contain these parts of me, it made my bond with God unsound
Thus all my guilt was less than likely to attain, a worthy penance to be found

I knew how much the devil's charm had cuckolded me, beguiling me from stem to stern
For vanity was man's true soul, a state of mind subconsciously to which we yearn

216

It wasn't just enough that I must struggle gainst the rigors
that our lives require
But knowing I must answer for my choices made, left me
more sunken in the mire

As time would stretch my troubled heart, I knew that it
would slowly pass each year by year
Yet moodiness still pressed on me, from knowing that my
children longed to have me near

The road I paved was not the best, but over time had forti-
fied in steadiness
For we sustained the bedrock of our kinship bond, and trav-
eled this in thankfulness

Hence time rolled by as I performed parental tasks, of love
and guidance, and advice
And watched my children grow and grow, becoming more so
special in their own device

These were the years I basked within those tender joys,
together with my Clementine
For we engaged in such adventures and good times, that
only God was more divine

But of the love I've always sought, had never been more
deeply than what I have now
For I was blessed these many years to have someone who I
adored, and would take vow

Thus as the years enriched our lives, we settled on
the peaks of all our happiness
And found a tract of perfect balance was attained, that
bound us closer, I confess

Yet comforts of that rosy age played me the fool, for troubles
loomed right down the road
With time in flight a hoary shift befell my mask, as health
now waned to life's hard load

Although the wages owed to her were not that steep, as all
my steps still had some stride
It would just be the onset of tomorrow's reign, which slowly
sped us to her side

The children were no longer that, and had now reached an youthful age within their prime
And marched unto their chosen beat, with boundless point of views that fill their hearts and time

Such were the years upon me now, handcuffed by faults, and sold to bondage to my sin
And found myself redundantly failing, as efforts to repent would ne'er begin

I did my best in that dual time, between the needs of others and my ebbing self
And came to see a simple truth, that I could not keep pace with all I gave myself

Then came the day I've always longed, when all my years at work had earned an ending vent
Allowing me to have at last the golden years, my long awaited retirement

This was the dream of all good souls, to thumb their nose forever more at any work
For it was now a slow down time, a time to settle back and let the clock hand lurk

But woe to an age past it's time, for this was when the scourge of death came to hover
As would my father come to see his midnight hour, a soul the angels would recover

Thus fared this kind and loving man, who's now been released into the vaults of heaven
A loss driven deep by the pangs of my sorrow, as he sails home to his brethren

But my pain was more than a heart feeling broken, twas another grave problem too
For time's gruff hand had cowed the flesh, and exhausted the avenues my heart pushed through

Hence now, I too, stood on death's porch, for potent was the gravity of my new woe
And waited at God's unfathomable pleasure, while the surgeons readied to go

In the days that I've spent in waiting to be seen, played hard
on my nerves and my heart
To know nothing in how my surgery would fare, made
anxiousness harder to part

Over the years I have shied from facing my guilt, from sins
and what I've failed to do
And always I have known that the day would soon come,
when I must face this issue through

Then came my chance to set things right, to what shame
and reluctance had seeded in me
To finally at last find unyielding courage, from a priest who
had set me free

There're some who'd say, that heaven's bounds will all
depend, on confessing to all your sins
But the details given, weigh less of importance, as intent to
not sin again

God's gracious light now glowed again, as his undaunted
spirit bestirred me once more
By decisively filling my heart with his strength, to what
ending he had in store

So now that I have the Lord's mercy and blessing, with my
tears attesting to that
No more shall I worry of his righteous disdain, the weight's
now his, where sins are at

So now I wait that given time, when I must face that ghostly
moment by design
When mortal flesh must cheat the hand of sneaky death, if
God's desire and mine align

Hence came the morning's gentle eve, when I succumbed to
those last thoughts before the wend
And gave them to the Lord of hosts, as well as all the trust I
felt, that I won't end

Thus fell the dark, where darkness reign, a darken sleep
that held itself so darkly deep
That gave to me no part to hold, no dream, or thought, or
sense of bodhi, that I could keep

And seemed to last mere seconds only in my lapse, before
sensation chose to stay
As all good people to my health, performed the needed
duties that would help this day

Such was the feeble consciousness, aware of their attentive-
ness on my behalf
Until at last I had returned, and now could freely interact
with all the staff

Although my mien may not reflect, inside I felt the joy of
having seen it through
To thus endure 'la mort respire,' and then regain the bound-
aries that mortals hew

It was to God that this went well, and helped by all those
offered prayers voiced to thee
For providence had paved my way, and I was blessed to have
so many care for me

So grateful was my new healed heart, to everyone who called
to God to ease my way
But greater yet was thankfulness to him above, who
deemed that I shall live today

And thus did time resume its march, ascending me into her
future depths and turns
Which brought me home where I belong, to doting friends
and family, and love adjourns

As better days would drift on by, my health improved, as
would my spirit's point of view
For bonds between my loving kin had taken strength, but
with my children, more than true

My mind was now quite firmly set, that I would hold myself
onto a greater bent
To stay there on this course I set, by giving God devotedness
in full extent

Thus as my days progressed to months, I found myself still
more involved in better ways
And even though I savored church, great strides were made
to stand and face confession's gaze

For all my life I've never really had control, on all the things
I've ever said
And heedlessly spat hateful words, with other foul indecen-
cies, when anger led

This truth I've claimed of spoken words, which never can be
hidden from the ears of God
Are always there to rise again, displaying all our wickedness
at heaven's nod

For I at last with lesson learned, now strive to hold my
tongue in check, to what I say
Since all the hurt that I had caused throughout my years, is
never fully washed away

They simply are immutable, and only features all the scars
my words begat
Hence being why one reason for my penitence, to cleanse my
soul for doing that

So hear this truth I give to you, that when you seek forgive-
ness from whom it is due
Make sure that you forgive yourself, for it will be the hardest
thing you'll ever do

For those who truly feel ashamed from what they've done,
will always feel this timeless guilt
And want this more than anything, because they held them-
selves within a cell they built

But I at last have been set free, foremost by God in humble
course of sacrament
And then by me, who've always let my shame and guilt
control my will, from what was meant

No more will I be hanging on that cross I built, where fear
and time had driven me
For I now stand at my new post, and will defend this solemn
mount so stringently

Behold this newly given world, a life that I now understand
more fully well
That lies at best south of heaven, but ever more so near in
lying north of hell